APR 2 5 2016

HERITAGE BUILDERS

SIR WHITE HOUSE CHEF

Dr. Ronnie Seaton, Author

Dr. Sherman Smith, Co-Author

HERITAGE BUILDERS PUBLISHING
MONTEREY, CLOVIS CALIFORNIA

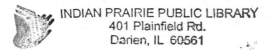

HERITAGE BUILDERS

First Edition 2015

Edited by Dr. Sherman Smith
Cover Design by Rae House, Creative Marketing
Book Design by Keith Bennett
Published by Heritage Builders Publishing
Clovis, California 93619
Monterey, California 93940
www.HeritageBuilders.com 1-888-898-9563

ISBN 978-1941437-93-3

PRINTED AND BOUND IN THE
UNITED STATES OF AMERICA

HERITAGE BUILDERS

This book contains the story and history as told by
Sir Master Chef Dr. Ronnie Seaton, Sr. The opinions expressed
are his own, and not necessarily those of Dr. Sherman Smith
or Heritage Builders Publishing, LLC.

DEDICATION

Dedicated to my Grandmother Willie Mae Seaton.

July 16, 1916 – September 18, 2015.

She was the Owner and Chef of the World Famous
Willie Mae Scotch House Restaurant,
New Orleans, Louisiana.

TABLE OF CONTENTS

ACKNOWLEDGEMENTS

For my wife, Dr. Ann Sheffield-Seaton.

My father and mother, Charles W. Seaton and
Doris Parker-Seaton.

My grandmothers Mrs. Willie Mae Seaton and
Mrs. Beaulah Parker.

My mother-in-law Mrs. Loretta Young-Sheffield.

And of course my children, my grandchildren,
and my dear friends.

Dr. Sherm Smith, my Publisher and Writer,
who believed in this project.

Eric O'Neal, Grand Master and 7 times undefeated
World Karate Champion, who encouraged me to sign my
contract with Heritage Builders Publishing.

FORWARD

by Dr. Ann Seaton

Cooking to Please, I bring the restaurant to you!

For many years, Ronnie Seaton has been passion driven by his love for cooking. His warm personality, knowledge, and hard work have been experienced through his delectable cuisine whether cooking for a President or making a wonderful dinner for this family.

For many years, Ronnie has envisaged social change by creating a culinary school for young children. His persistence, perseverance, and most importantly, his strong faith in God has made his dreams attainable. He has recently launched two programs one entitled, "Commis Culinary Café and Cooking to Please."

For many years, Ronnie's destiny as a chef has been greatly influenced by his grandmother Willie Mae Seaton, who was both the culinarian and the matriarch of the family. Growing up in a family that thrives on hard work, rich traditions, and culinary history has instilled that passion in Ronnie. Similar to his grandmother, he too will be an exemplar for the new generation of chefs.

For many years, Ronnie has been a wonderful husband, father, mentor, and puissant advocate for education. My husband has been my greatest support in pursuing my Ph.D. – A journey that has been both rewarding and challenging.

I love you and wish you much success, Ann.

SIR WHITE HOUSE CHEF

CHAPTER ONE
The Early Years

I am Ronnie Seaton, and I was born May 4, 1955 to Charles Seaton and Doris Parker two years after they were married. My father was twenty years old, and my mother was eighteen. I grew up on 2318 South Galvis Street in New Orleans, Louisiana.

I was born into a very strict religious family, and my grandmother made sure I went to church. She made me attend Saint Monica's Catholic Church, Stroke of Hope Baptist Church, and Ebenezer Baptist Church. I went to church from morning to night on Sundays so my grandmother knew where I was at all times.

I attended a very strong Catholic School taught by Blessed Sacrament Nuns and Josephite Priests. I became an altar boy when I was in the fourth grade and continued serving in that role in my church for four years. Every single year, I was the "Altar Boy of the Year." The Priests honored me with the award because I was always on time and took my job very seriously.

I was very respectful of the Priests. The Priests never molested, and they taught us strong morals and values and so did the Nuns.

As a child, I had a fascination for what was happening in the kitchen of our somewhat modest and crowded home. That passion came from my grandmother on my mother's side. She cooked for the nuns at the Catholic School where I attended, and my other grandmother on my father's side opened a restaurant. All this activity involving the preparation of food was bound to have an impact on my young life.

While at Saint Monica Church, I attended Saint Augusta High

School that was an all white school. I went there in 1968 and loved the "Purple Knights", the school's nickname. While in the ninth grade, I decided to join the early junior seminarians because I had the desire and aspiration at that young age to be a priest.

My dad and mom and both grandmothers thought it was a great thing that their boy, much more mature than his age, wanted to serve God. I gave my life to this cause through the ninth and tenth grades. In the eleventh grade, I had an aberration that mixed up my thinking. One day the head Priest called me into his office. I had never been summoned by a priest to have a one on one conversation, so as I stood there facing my fate, I nervously fidgeted with both hands in my pockets.

"Master Ronnie, you are going to have to give up dating girls." The Priest instructed me sternly.

Without blinking an eye or even praying about it, I cried out, "Father, I can't do that. I like girls way too much."

When I got home that afternoon and told the news to my parents and grandmothers, they were very disappointed and tried to talk me into giving up dating, so I could become a priest.

I thought long and hard about this and told them later that evening, "I like girls, and I am not going to be a priest."

Towards the end of my senior year in high school, this boy who was the only son and had flat feet, got a draft notice stating that I was going to Vietnam.

"What!" I exclaimed. "I am the only child, and I am not supposed to be going to war."

I graduated from high school in the top five percent of my class and had a scholarship to attend Howard University where I planned at that young age to become a doctor.

All plans were put on hold as I said goodbye to my girlfriend, Ann Sheffield, and headed off to basic training because the Army would have its way. When I got my first leave of absence, I came home to Ann and asked her to marry me. She turned me down.

"Why won't you marry me?" I cried.

"I'm seventeen years old." Ann replied. "I can't marry you."

I was beside myself and wouldn't take "no" for an answer. I headed over to her parents house and asked her mom and dad.

"You can marry our daughter," her father said, "but you have to wait until she is eighteen."

That made me very happy because in three weeks from that day, Ann would be eighteen. In four weeks, I came home on a pass, dressed in my blues, bought a marriage license, and sought out a Josephite Priest. We got married in front of the whole church.

My dad put down a broom, and the bride and groom jumped over to the sound of a Howitzer shot off by one of my army buddies, who came down with me to witness the marriage, and then we took off on a one day honeymoon.

I left my bride and returned to the duties as a soldier at AIT in Augusta, Georgia and then the Army, as they promised, sent me all the way to Vietnam. Soon after I arrived, I got a letter in the mail that would change my life.

I forgot to tell you, Ann Seaton wrote. *I am pregnant.*

When it came time for Ann to have the baby, the Red Cross paid my way home. I arrived there in time for the birth of the baby, and then two days after the baby was born, I had to return to Vietnam.

CHAPTER ONE
Vietnam POW

Ten days after I was in Vietnam, I got captured. I was only eighteen, and I was ordered as an African American to the body bag detail. This job required the soldiers to find the dead bodies of their fellow men and place them in body bags to be shipped home. Truly one of the most grievous jobs in the Army was bagging the bodies of these men who died for their country. I never looked at the job as degrading but rather faced those days with dignity like I had everything else in life.

My troop was on detail. We were moving along the tree line when suddenly we came upon many dead snakes. I thought, *something ain't right.* Often when the boys bagged bodies that were missing their heads, snakes would come out of the orifices where they had been hiding. One of these snakes had bitten me on the butt, and it took a lot of antibiotics to keep me from dying from the infection the non-venomous snake inflicted on me.

A young recent graduate of West Point had ordered our troops to walk down a road when we were far away from our base camp instead of pushing through the brush out of sight.

A Sergeant working with the troops told the Lieutenant that we were exposing ourselves to danger. This did not deter the young officer to maintain his order.

Who do I listen to? I thought. *I am only a private.*

All of us obeyed the orders of the recent West Point grad and maintained our position moving down the middle of the road. Soon we came on dead bodies, so we prepared ourselves to tag the bodies, bag them, and send them home. Soon, we spotted a body, and the Lieutenant ordered the body to be tagged and bagged.

"Lieutenant, don't go over by that body," the Sergeant exclaimed.

"Why?" The Lieutenant replied.

"That body's booby trapped."

"How do you know?"

"Because I know!" The Sergeant yelled.

One of the soldiers listened to the order of the Lieutenant and to the horror of the other six men on the patrol, the body exploded and took the life of this young American soldier.

"Dogs – get down!" The Vietcong yelled as they popped out of the trenches.

My best friend, who had hesitated, was shot and killed in cold blood while standing beside me. When the Vietcong captors told all the troops to stand up with our hands on top of our heads, all of us smitten soldiers were escorted to a prisoner of war camp where we would spend the rest of the war if we survived.

Every day was hell on earth for us prisoners. Each morning, the Vietcong would wake all the soldiers and subject us to a severe beating. During this time of punishment, the Vietcong put sacks on the heads of us kids, urinated on us, and then beat on us some more. This went on every day we were in the POW camp. I survived the ordeal by finding comfort and hope as I stared at the photos of my wife and baby that I had hidden in my shoe.

One of those brutal days, they killed my high school classmate. At only eighteen years old, I thought my opportunity for survival would never come and like my friend, I would die a cruel death.

I spent my time in a crate that was akin to a dog cage. Regularly, we would have hoods placed over our heads, so that we couldn't see our captors and were then beaten like the dogs the Vietcong claimed we were. They smeared feces on our faces, and urinated on us before the hoods were placed over our heads. The smell inside those hot stinking hoods was nauseating.

"Tell us the plans of your Army!" The Vietcong soldier screamed at me.

They had gotten mad at me for something I had said to one of the camp guards. I would give no information except my name, rank, and serial number. I wouldn't tell them what they wanted to know, so they shot me in the knee.

The bullet did not exit the knee and bled and bled. The Sergeant tied a tourniquet around my leg to stop the blood from flowing. No pain medicine or antibiotics were given to help the situation, so this was a cruel, cruel place that I, an eighteen year old man-child, had found myself. Today I have braces on my legs and cannot drive a car because of the cruel treatment the Vietcong forced the "Nigger-dogs" to endure.

The Vietcong had taken the dog tags from each of the soldiers but let us keep our chains. When this happened, the Sergeant realized that the Vietcong didn't know that they had inadvertently given their prisoners a saw.

Every night, the soldiers would urinate on the bamboo poles holding the fortress together and would then cut a little with our makeshift saw.

During storms, we would kick and weaken the buttress little by little. On the twenty-first day of our capture, we broke free. The Lieutenant, who had caused us to be in this terrible situation in the first place, kept trying to get us to negotiate. The Sergeant maintained that we did not negotiate with the enemy, and that we were getting out of there as fast as we could.

When the Vietcong realized we had gotten ourselves free, they took after us in hot pursuit. I was wounded, ragged and having a difficult time keeping up. It was right before our capture a second time, and one we surely would not survive, that we ran into a platoon of Army Rangers doing reconnaissance behind the enemy lines. They quickly secured us prisoners and got us out of harm's way.

CHAPTER ONE
My Whole World Changed

I was sent back to the States but not yet discharged from the Service. I used this time recuperating to earn two college degrees in Management and Accounting.

One day I picked up Time Magazine that had a chef on the front cover, and I began perusing the pages. There was an article entitled *Doctors and Lawyers Becoming Chefs.* The article pointed to two schools that were offering degrees in Culinary Arts – Johnson and Wells and Culinary Institute of America in Hyde Park, New York. I took the time to write to both schools, and the Culinary Institute of America sent a plane ticket to me.

I was discharged from the Army after serving eight years. My rank was E7, and I had been decorated with the Purple Heart and the Bronze Star. I was the youngest recruit to earn that rank as a non-commissioned officer. I was thinking heavily about staying in the Service but when they told me they were sending me to Turkey, I decided I did not want to be away from my family again, so I received an Honorable Discharge.

I chose to attend the Culinary Institute of America because my Godmother lived nearby, and I could stay with her while I was going through school. I would be offered a scholarship if I could bake an apple pie that the chefs at the school would love. I returned home to New Orleans, and my grandmother, Ms. Willie Mae Seaton, gave me an old time southern recipe for apple pie. Granny Smith apples, a crust made from buttermilk, butter, eggs (brown eggs), flour, baking soda, baking powder, sugar, brown sugar, vanilla, and baked in a deep dish. The Culinary Institute awarded it number one, and I received a scholarship.

When it was time for me to complete my internship, a friend, Veronica Swartz, who everybody called Ronnie, and I received our assignments. Veronica was going to New Orleans, and I was headed to San Diego. Somehow, the orders got mixed up, and I was sent to New Orleans, and Ronnie Swartz to San Diego. Once we realized the mix-up, neither of us said anything to anybody and left for our respective assignments in the two cities.

I was assigned a post under Chef Leon West, who was the Executive Corporate Chef for Air Mark, and was my mentor while I was at the Convention Center in New Orleans.

I was older than the other students, who were completing their coursework, but I was very disciplined, a character trait that served me well then and in the future. One day, Chef Leon introduced me to all the chefs working in the center. The entire crew was white, and they were all graduates of Johnson and Wells and didn't like graduates of Culinary Institute.

They set me up one afternoon when I was supposed to chop up four cases of bell peppers. One of the chefs changed the order and put a "0" behind the 4, so I thought that I had to chop up 40 cases by myself. I did this and when Chef Leon inspected the food, he was amazed that 40 cases were chopped instead of four. When he asked me why I chopped 40 instead of four, I told him that was the number on the order.

Chef Leon then forced the jokesters to admit their prank, and then he made me in charge of all those white chefs. His first order was to have me make them clean the entire kitchen with toothbrushes. It took them two days.

Later, these six white chefs became my friends and respected me. We did many events together including the one meal that cost $1,000,000.00 for the Nissan Corporation that went into the Guinness Book of Records as the most expensive meal for forty thousand people. I put together the game plan that would pull off this record setting feat; one meal for one million dollars.

I was going to complete my internship in two months because I worked twenty hours a day. I would go home and sleep for three hours and then clean up and go back to work. I would be at work at 4:00 a.m. and work until midnight.

After being there for almost two months, it was announced that President Ronald Reagan was coming to New Orleans, and that he was going to have a private dinner at the convention center for one hundred people.

Because I was so disciplined and had the respect of Chef Leon West, the chef gave me the opportunity to cook for one hundred financial supporters at a cost of one thousand dollars a plate. I was in the center for three days with the Secret Service. Before I could start the dinner, the Secret Service were checking everything in the kitchen, dining areas and even went to my house and my parent's home. After a clean slate, they declared me okay to cook for the President.

I was a new kid on the block, so I began an exercise regimen that would get me in the best shape of my life. Push-ups, pull-ups, sit-ups, and running were my daily routine as I attacked this chore like a prizefighter going for a title.

I said an emotional "goodbye" to Ann and told her I would meet her in two weeks. I literally lived at the convention center because there was no way I was going to mess up this unique and special opportunity.

I began practicing the meal. I would make the courses over and over and even had the spinach leaves the exact same size. I made all the sauces while the Secret Service observed and tasted everything I made. Later they would abandon the "tasting" because of the dangers but at that time, they were still in the practice as part of protecting the Presidents' lives. I still remembers that day like it was yesterday.

The first course was a spinach salad with strawberries soaked in vinaigrette, blueberries from Slidell, Louisiana, toasted pine nuts from Egypt to the color of peanut butter and feta cheese also from a farm in Slidell, Louisiana. I made the raspberry vinaigrette dressing from scratch.

The second course was French onion soup with Black Angus beef tips, beef broth, red onions and French bread with melted mozzarella cheese on top. White wine and Sherry were mixed in the soup.

The third course was a blood orange sorbet prepared to cleanse the pallet before the entrée was served.

The main course was lamb chops flown in from Australia stuffed with Louisiana crabmeat. The Duchess potatoes were Yukon Gold potatoes from the Jacqueline Kennedy era. They were made with heavy cream, nutmeg, white pepper, French butter, and mashed through a ricer, put in a pacer bag, piped out, egg washed, and baked a second time to look like a rosette. The vegetable was white asparagus with a béarnaise sauce made fresh with tarragon and white wine.

One of Reagan's favorite desserts was bananas foster. I made up my own recipe that contained French butter, light brown sugar, vanilla, cinnamon, and nutmeg all mixed together. Bananas are cut into four pieces with banana liqueur, 151 rum and Madagascar vanilla. I served it over vanilla ice cream. I lighted the masterpiece up and as the flames heated it, I threw sparkling cinnamon on it and yelled, "C'est," which means, "that's it!"

I presented this meal to the President and his guests in such an artistic fashion that it resembled the corsage on a woman's dress.

I was an apprentice chef working by myself in this kitchen with no help and cooking for one hundred people. I looked to the Secret Service for help, but they didn't lift a finger.

I set the table *alone*. I placed a golden charger on the table. I then placed a salad plate, soup bowl, a bread and butter plate with the butter pats made into rosettes. Next came the entrée plate, dessert bowl, and the last pieces of flatware were coffee spoon, soup spoon, entrée knife, entrée fork, salad fork, and dessert spoon. Last came the coffee saucer with the coffee cup placed with the handle at the five o'clock position because the President was right handed. A water goblet, a glass for white wine, red wine, and champagne completed the table setting.

"This beautiful table arrangement was only the beginning of the talents this young energetic chef would bring to the enjoyment of those Ronnie will serve for a lifetime." This was said of me at a benefit dinner held in my honor.

The centerpiece was an arrangement of red roses, white carnations, and blue irises set only eighteen inches off the table, so the person's view across the table was not blocked. The napkin ring was Mother of Pearl. The linen napkins were folded to look like a fleur-de-lis. The tablecloth had a gold lace with a gold under lay, and I designed and constructed this masterpiece by myself. It took me two days to set the table using a ruler to make sure the setting was perfect. This habit of working so hard would define who I would become as those I served would benefit so much.

After hours of hard work, the meal was finally ready, and I was led down a hallway to a private dining room. Ronald Reagan was coming down the hallway, and I asked the Secret Service if I could get President Reagan's autograph. I was told in no uncertain terms not to approach the President.

There were waiters moving the food to the tables, and President Reagan walked by where I was standing while presenting his food.

"Chef, what do we have here?" President Reagan asked me.

"Mr. President, this is the meal," and I told him what I had prepared. "Mr. President, can I have your autograph?" I boldly asked while the Secret Service cleared their throats.

"Chef, I will be out in twenty-eight minutes, and I'll come to see you." The President grinned.

Exactly twenty-eight minutes later, the President came out of the dining area and walked straight to me.

"This is the best meal I've ever had," said the President.

"Are you sure?" I asked.

"I will not lie to you," said the President. "Would you like to come to the White House?"

SECTION I
PRESIDENT RONALD REAGAN

CHAPTER ONE
Starting the Career

President Reagan meant business when he asked me to come to the White House.

"But Mr. President," I said, "I can't come see the White House. I have two weeks of school left."

"You don't understand," the President replied, " I want you *working* in the White House, and you have thirty minutes to make up your mind. Call your wife."

I rushed to the nearest phone and called Annie.

"Where you been, Ronnie?" Ann asked with some disdain in her voice.

"I have to ask you something, Annie, so listen to me. I have been cooking for the President."

"The President of what?" Ann asked skeptically.

"Of the U-N-I-T-E-D S-T-A-T-E-S!"

"Stop the BS, Ronnie, this ain't funny."

"The President wants us to come to the White House and work in the kitchen, and I need you to understand what this means." I pleaded.

"What do you say, Ronnie?"

"I say we're going." I replied with no hesitation in my voice.

I received their clearances and headed to Washington, D.C. after the President had influenced the Culinary Institute of America to graduate me with honors two weeks early. This was a request the school was most happy to comply.

White House chefs must have top-secret clearances, and I

found myself going through an ordeal. I was drug tested, finger printed, and my head and eyeballs were scanned.

When the background checks were finished concerning my family, my aunt was not cleared to come to the White House. It seems that she had a gambling problem and owed casinos gambling debts. Because of this, she was banned from ever coming to the White House. This was a situation that caught Ann and me completely off guard, and the reality and gravity of the new career on which we were embarking took on a sense of extreme seriousness.

I started working for President Reagan in Kitchen 3 – this is the kitchen that makes the food for the State Department. It is a Piccadilly Cafeteria style restaurant with a Ruth's Chris Steakhouse menu. The workers in the State Department go through a line and order what they want put on their plates, then sit and eat.

I worked as a Type 3 Chef the entire time that Ronald Reagan was President. I did everything they wanted me to do and did it well. I prepped food and worked aggressively for long hours, which would ultimately serve me well.

Soon I was noticed for my untiring commitment. I didn't want to remain only a servant; I wanted to move up. I was not as young as many of the cooks who worked with me, so I started applying for every certification test I could qualify for as fast as I could. I passed through these exams rapidly and received certifications one on top of the other until I became the Executive Chef of Kitchen 3.

One of the highlights of my career was when I passed and received notice that my chef status had changed, and I had been approved as the Executive Chef. I was delighted one evening when President Ronald Reagan entered the kitchen unannounced but not unnoticed. In the President's hands was the certification document that I had earned. No one had ever heard of before or since a President going to one of the White House Kitchens to present a certification to a chef. "Goosebumps ran up and down my spine."

Afterwards, President Reagan would inquire about me and how I was doing. It seemed he had a special place in his heart for this African American chef serving the State Department employees.

One day, President Reagan sent an unprecedented memo by one of the White House staff runners that he wanted Chef Ronnie Seaton in Kitchen 3 to prepare his lunch.

I never forgot that special day in my life. I loved the President who had so graciously befriended me. I remember so well the first lunch meal I made for President Reagan.

I took the lunch to the Oval Office where I'd never been and in my possession was the food the President requested.

When I walked in, I was surprised to find that no one was in the office except the President and me. I stood there with the table of food I had pushed through those hallowed halls, and now I was one on one with the President of the United States of America.

"What do you have there chef?" The President asked.

"Well, Mr. President, I have made a garden salad with heirloom tomatoes topped with a creamy ranch dressing for starters. You will have a New York strip steak cooked medium rare and a twice-baked potato on the side with Brussell sprouts as your vegetable. Of course, I have made oatmeal cookies to eat with your vanilla ice cream and topped it with fresh strawberries."

After I had presented the food one course at a time, the President finished his last drop of coffee and with half a smile he asked me,

"Chef Seaton, where are the jellybeans?"

Was the chef in trouble? Not on your life was he. I reached and pulled a small dish from under a white cloth napkin, and jellybeans were neatly placed in a pattern that could have been from a kaleidoscope. I handed the beans to the President.

President Ronald Reagan was known for his affinity of a certain jellybean made by a factory named Jelly Belly, which is located in Fairfield, California about an hour's drive from San Francisco.

I am proud to say that I made my President proud. Not only did I remember the President's favorite candy, but I had done my research.

"Mr. President, those are peanut butter and jelly jellybeans. I believe they are your favorite."

The President smiled and then patted me on the shoulder and said, "Welcome to my world of work."

"Mr. President, this is not work. It is my love and my passion."

The President smiled.

CHAPTER TWO
Nancy Reagan

Of all the First Ladies that I would work with, Nancy Reagan was by far the most difficult. The only way to describe her is as a "Drill Sergeant."

One of her most stringent exercises concerning the kitchens was when there was an event at the White House. She would walk around with a ruler and a piece of string. Everything involved in the presentations by the chefs had to be measured to the maximum tolerance.

Nancy ran the kitchen like a military regiment. She would walk around with a white glove on her hand and use her finger to check for dust. She was the First Lady extraordinaire. She kept a tight rein on everything President Reagan was involved in and would never take a chance that he would be embarrassed for any reason.

The first president to ever wear a brown suit was President Reagan, and Nancy is the one who picked the suit and the white shirt he wore with it.

She wanted him to look good, so she insisted that he dye his hair, which he did.

When there was a state dinner, no First Lady could dress like Nancy Reagan. She wanted everything perfect including herself. She in no way wanted to ever do anything that would embarrass her country or her President.

One time she walked up to me and asked, "How's Ann doing. How are the boys doing?"

"Mrs. Reagan, how do you know my wife?" I asked incredulously.

"I know everything about you," she replied. "I'm going to the boys' school next week."

"Why? What have they done?"

"They've done nothing," she replied. "I want to bring something to the kids at school, and I want your boys to receive it."

The Reagans were famous for doing things like that just out of the clear blue and surprising everyone.

Now and then, the President would want to dine privately with his First Lady. I almost always got the call to make the dinner. One such time after they had dined, the President asked that I remain in the room. He then told the Secret Service agent nearby to have some music piped into the room.

Soon the soft music was playing, and the President and Nancy Reagan danced slowly in front of me. When they stopped dancing, they turned toward me and clapped acknowledging their appreciation for my dedication and commitment to making sure that the President and the First Lady were treated to world class dinners prepared by this African American chef from New Orleans.

CHAPTER THREE
Reflections

I will make no apologies about maintaining who my favorite President is. "Ronald Reagan is my favorite President,"

Not only was President Ronald Reagan my favorite President, but I believe I was President Reagan's favorite chef. The President never hid from anyone his love for me and afforded me privileges never before seen with chefs working in the third kitchen.

One of the favorite memories about President Reagan that impressed me was his ability to work a speech without a teleprompter.

He didn't need one. He was an actor, so he was comfortable talking to anyone, and he talked to the American people like they were his next door neighbors.

The habits of the Presidents were common knowledge throughout the White House staff, and the Secret Service and the kitchen staff were in constant chit chat with one another all the time. The Secret Service guys would come into the kitchen, and they would spread the gossip. There was always a close relationship with the Secret Service and the kitchens. They all knew each other well.

One of the things that fostered a lot of gossip was the affair's the Presidents had. It is difficult to have a secret affair in the White House when you are the President of the United States. I stayed clear of all that, and I didn't want to hear about it because it was none of my business.

President Reagan loved horses, so the kitchen was constantly involved in "cook outs," and the President loved dressing in jeans and western clothes. He had many pairs of cowboy boots and he wore the same size as me. One day, President Reagan gave a pair of his boots to me which I still have to this day.

The consensus of a lot of people in the United States at the time of the Reagan Presidency was that Ronald Reagan was too old to be the President. He was, after all, the oldest President to take the Oval Office. One of the kitchen's favorite pastimes was to reflect on the fact that the President had a memory as keen as anybody could imagine, and this thought of his age and memory was a hoax. The President hardly met a person on his staff whose name he didn't remember, and when he walked into a room, he would greet his staff by their first names. He called me, "Ronnie." The President made you feel like he'd known you his entire life. He had a keen sense of humility and was as personable as if he was your best friend, and that is why the White House staff loved him whether in the kitchen or cleaning the floors.

After our second child was born, President Reagan made a personal visit to the hospital to visit the mother and the newborn babe. No President that I served was known to take that kind of interest in a kitchen staff member.

You just don't see this happen, and when I think about it, my eyes tear up, and I have to choke back the emotions. The First Lady accompanied the President and brought flowers and a teddy bear. We were overwhelmed.

If you visit our home, one of the first things you will spot is the little gray teddy sitting proudly by Ronald and Nancy Reagan's picture.

President Ronald Reagan saw no color in people, and he loved people. He told me on many occasions that he could never forget the people who bought tickets to his movies and made him a star, or the people who put him in office. There was no mistake that he was a most dedicated human being that happened to be the President of the United States.

I respected the President's ability to talk about any subject he found interesting. He was an actor, athlete, politician, but above all a Statesman no matter what a person's personal opinion of him was. Not once in the seven years that I worked in Kitchen 3 at the White House did I ever see President Ronald Reagan disrespect anyone.

I worked in Kitchen 3, but President Reagan would ask me to be moved at times to cook with the chefs in Kitchen 1 that was the kitchen responsible for what the President and his guests would eat.

The first time I was asked to move from my place in Kitchen 3 and report to Kitchen 1 was a shock to me. When I received the order and tried to get some advice, no one in my kitchen had any experience working in Kitchen 1, so I labored and stressed over the situation to the point that I almost became ill.

I was the new chef on the block, so I marched up to Kitchen 1 and poked my head in the door. I was greeted by a couple of cooks, who satisfied their curiosity as to who this new chef was that was getting so much attention. They had never seen an Afro-American chef called up from the State Department kitchen to Kitchen 1 to specifically prepare a meal for the President of the United States.

"Hi, I'm Chef Ronnie Seaton," I said as I stuck out my hand. "Why am I here?"

The Master Chef of Kitchen 1 politely replied, "You are ordered to prepare a meal for the President of the United States at his request."

My mouth literally fell open, my jaw dropped, and I gasped for air. A heaviness fell into my chest, and my heart was in my stomach.

"What kind of meal?" I nervously asked.

"Something from New Orleans," the Master Chef replied to the chuckles from the staff working beside him.

President Reagan loved Jambalaya, Gumbo, and one of his favorite foods was Etouffee. Etouffee is a spicy dish typically of shellfish over rice and employs a technique called "smothering." Smothering is cooking in a covered pan with low heat and a little liquid. The President loved this meal but preferred deer meat to shellfish. President Reagan didn't like rice, so it was replaced with a sweet potato biscuit, and deer meet cooked over the potato.

I was privileged to cook many of these meals for the President, and another of his favorites was fried alligator. I made this special delicacy with remoulade sauce and stuffed the meat inside an onion. Remoulade is made with a mayonnaise and ketchup base, garlic, horseradish, black pepper, red pepper, and white wine. It is a recipe unique to New Orleans.

President Reagan's favorite dessert was a dark chocolate cake with a ganache icing. This delicious topping is made with heavy cream, and melted Belgium chocolate. The strawberries in the side dish were always imported from California. The berries along with other fruit from California were special ordered and flown especially for the President's dining pleasures. All champagnes were flown in from California as well as the other wines.

I fell in love with Julia Child when she visited the White House. She was invited by the President and First Lady along with Jacques Pepin an internationally famous chef as Julia Child is. Both of these recognized stars of the kitchen were Master Chefs.

Julia and Jacques arrived in the kitchen with quite some fanfare. The cooks and other staff members in the kitchens were enamored by these famous people, and I was no exception. Both Master Chefs immediately liked me and took me under their wings. They recognized I had a talent for preparing delightful and delicious food.

The visiting chefs were in Kitchen 1 for one reason and one reason only; they were preparing a meal for the President of the United States and his guests. I was invited to stand along side Julia Child and Jacques Pepin, and an event I will remember and talk about for the rest of my life.

We prepared salmon with capers, caviar on toast points, escargot, and lobster with clarified butter.

Julia Child taught me how to make crème brule.

I then came up with my own recipe that I use all the time. Crème brule with golden raspberries on the bottom. You make the custard without any yoke from the eggs. The ramekins used for cooking the dessert are baked in a pan with water about half way up the bowl, so that you don't scorch the bottom of the dish. Raw sugar from Louisiana is placed on top of the custard, and then a blowtorch is fired up and used to harden the sugar into a delicious coating. I would then make chocolate feathers and place them in the dish and hit them with a little nitrogen to freeze the chocolate. Taking your spoon to dip down through the sugar to the bottom and spoon up those golden raspberries is so delicious it's hard to explain.

President Reagan also loved hamburgers and every time he wanted one, I would make one for him. I cooked most all of the hamburgers the President ate during the entire time I served him.

I believe I won the President over with my own special hamburger recipe that President Reagan loved. It was made with Gouda cheese in the middle of two patties. The meat had to be ground up fresh with garlic, and then the two patties were put into a press that made them perfectly round while squishing the cheese perfectly to the edges. The patties were placed on a six-inch home made sesame seed toasted bun that had been spread with aioli, which is a marinated mayonnaise. Boston bib lettuce, heirloom tomatoes, and two raw red onion rings were placed on the top patty. The sandwich was then cut in half with a toothpick placed in each half.

This delicious American favorite was served with an order of oven baked steak fries. President Reagan did not like deep fried fries. I made my own spicy ketchup for dipping the fries.

For dessert, I would make the President an apple pie a la mode. Occasionally, the President would ask that his piece of apple pie be served with melted Swiss cheese on top instead of his favorite vanilla ice cream. I would make sure the melted cheese would drip over the sides of the pie.

President Ronald Reagan requested and ate this meal a minimum of three times every month that he was in office.

The first time the President ate this meal he said, "Ronnie you have a touch with food."

"Mr. President, you have a way with food," I replied. "You love what you eat, so I love what I do for you."

"Chef Ronnie, I have never seen a person like you. You work hard, you're always on time and never late." The President doted.

"Mr. President Sir, are you ever late?"

"The only way I would ever be late is if I was dead," the President said with his infectious smile.

President Reagan always wore the best suits and ties. His shoes shined like new money, and he polished each pair himself.

I love to reminisce about the upbringing of Ronald Reagan. He wasn't born rich with a silver spoon in his mouth like many Presidents were. He was poor, but he worked hard and made it all the way to the top position in the world. President Reagan said many times to me,

"I struggled, but I never gave up."

I could relate so well to what the President would share with me because from the time I knew that becoming a chef would be my passion, I wanted to be a chef in the White House.

I would dedicate myself to the man who hired me and gave me the dream of dreams. The President would call me at home in the night and would ask me for a favor.

"Ronnie," the President would say, "Could you do a little favor for me? Nancy has a little party she wants to throw for about twenty ladies, do you think you can handle it?"

"Mr. President, sir, when is it going to be?"

"Uh, tomorrow," the President replied.

I went over to the kitchen that afternoon on my day off to make sure that I had everything needed to make it the best party Nancy Reagan every threw.

The First Lady never measured me. She knew when she walked into the room everything would be perfect. There were twenty little old ladies in the room, and they had money. They were there to talk about issues, and what the First Lady needed to tell the President.

Nancy Reagan was known to pull the President's ear when she didn't like something. One day, she was especially aggravated as I was serving the President's lunch. Nancy walked in and strolled up to the President just as he was taking a bite of that juicy burger he loved so much.

"Ronnie," she said as she latched onto his ear pinching it between her thumb and index finger. " I told you that's no bill for you to sign."

The bill was on childcare. President Reagan changed his mind and vetoed the bill.

I did love the President. When President Reagan was shot, he requested that I come and visit him. This is a highly unusual event for a chef that is not at the top tier of the kitchen staff.

The President wanted certain soups and grilled cheese sandwiches with Canadian bacon delivered to his hospital room, and I would bring them. He wanted grilled marks on the bread, so I would take metal skewers and heat them to a temperature that they would make those grill marks on the bread.

"I hate this hospital food," the President told me on my first visit.

CHAPTER FOUR
Politics

I started voting at the age of eighteen years old and declared myself a Democrat. Ronald Reagan was a Republican President.

I never declared or claimed that I understood politics all that well and was never overly influenced by them.

I got along with President Reagan because I stayed away from politics, I know that in the military you serve your country and your president, so I decided when I began my career in the White House, I would serve the President.

Now and then the President would catch the kitchen staff lounging on the White House lawn, and he would walk up and ask them how they felt about things going on in the country like the economy.

The kitchen staff and the Secret Service were insulated from the influences that other people in the nation were experiencing because every thing was provided for them at the White House.

One of those days, the President surprised me lounging, so he walked up to me and ask me what would I like to talk about. I was living at the time in an area of Washington where the housing wasn't too great.

"Mr. President, what are you doing about affordable housing for the poor people?" I asked.

"Well, we're working on it," replied the President.

"Well, how long does it take to work on stuff?"

The President replied, "The wheels don't turn too fast. I have the Senate and the House of Representatives to work through before anything can move forward."

The kitchen staff was insulated for the most part from the government; even though they lived under the wing of all that was happening. One of the most exhilarating events for the entire staff was when President Ronald Reagan told the President of Russia, Mikhail Gorbachev, "Mr. Gorbachev tear down that wall."

I have never heard the White House personnel that were working that day cheer so loudly. You would think their team just won the Super Bowl.

When the President gave his State of the Union Address, the entire White House staff did not work during the speech. They would clap and cheer because this was their President, and they all loved him.

Politically, the President was colorblind. He staffed with every race and culture of the world. It didn't matter about the color of your skin; it did matter whether you could do the job.

I remember the day that President Reagan took his time from his very busy schedule and came to the kitchens to tell the staff what a magnificent job we did over the Christmas season. He was proud of us and let us know it. It was difficult work decorating for Christmas at the White House during Reagan's years because the ornaments were made of food.

The President threw a lot of parties at Christmas time. I was chosen twice towards the end of Ronald Reagan's term to make the food for some special guests who were large donors in the Presidents election campaigns.

Margaret Thatcher, England's Prime Minister, came to the White House at President Reagan's invitation. There was no doubt that Prime Minister Thatcher and President Ronald Reagan were soul mates. No one during the entire time that I served the President received so much respect and attention by the President.

The President called Kitchen 3 and wanted the Executive Chef. One of the jobs of the cooks for these dignitaries was to know before hand what their likes and dislikes were with the food they ate. I learned and would always do my research and because the President and First Lady trusted me, they left the preparation to me.

I always had the favorite recipes of these dignitaries in my hand but would add an extra twist to it.

After this special dinner prepared in honor of Prime Minister Thatcher, she asked the President who had prepared the meal. Immediately, President Reagan rang the kitchen and called for Chef Seaton to report to the White House dining area.

This little short black man came into the presence of the two most powerful political figures in the world at that time. Together, they had changed the course of history. I snapped to attention and after President Reagan introduced me to the Prime Minister as the chef who prepared the food, I bowed and showed my respect.

The next morning, President Reagan called me to the Oval Office.

"Ronnie, " the President said, "I never regret bringing you here."

"Mr. President, I've never regretted coming here."

There were only two chefs who attained the status with President Reagan that I had. The other was a German chef who could really bake. That chef was so skilled he could make a piece of paper taste good.

I also prepared the meals for Air Force One but at this time in my career, I was not advanced rank wise to the point where I could fly with the President.

Little containers of food were prepared for the meals and would be microwaved in the galley since there was no formal kitchen in Air Force One at that time. The President loved to wear a bomber jacket and eat his meals on the plane.

Mikhail Gorbachev, the last President of the Soviet Union, came to the White House. Gorbachev really liked President Ronald Reagan. The countries made it difficult for a President to have a good relationship with a Russian dignitary because of the Cold War.

President Reagan was his own man, so he put all that aside. During this visit, chefs brought food into the meeting between the two leaders.

When I brought in the food, my thought was that maybe I should get out of the room, or they should stop talking while I was in there. They didn't stop talking and ignored the fact I was in their presence. What I witnessed, I will never forget.

The President slammed his fist on the table and said, "Dammit Mikhail, you're going to do this or else!"

When the translator told Gorbachev what the President had said, Mr. Gorbachev nodded and said, "Okay, Mr. President."

Presidents of the United States entertain a lot of foreign dignitaries. In my opinion, it was the most important meal I made for any foreign dignitary. In fact, President Reagan came down to the kitchen later and applauded the chefs for such a fine presentation like he'd never seen before.

Food is an important element with highly profiled political meetings, and the meal that Gorbachev was served that night was unlike any he ever had in his life. The influence of the meal made Gorbachev change his mind or soften his opinion on some issues.

Gorbachev was really fond of President Reagan, and it was evident to all of the kitchen staff as well as others who worked at the White House. The Cold War kept the two presidential friends from having a complete relationship. President Reagan put these issues aside when he was having a meeting.

The first course of that historic dinner was a lump of crabmeat over Romaine lettuce. After this, a delicious Vichyssoise soup, which is a potato soup made with fresh cream. The German chef was mainly known for his ability to make world class pastries, but he could also make that soup better than anyone on the kitchen staff.

The main entrée was New York strip steak. Every piece of steak was cut to the same size of equal perfection. Pearl potatoes were served that were shaped like footballs, sautéed, and served with roasted onions mixed with asparagus.

Chocolate Mousse with a crème base on top was served for dessert. Afterwards, the Reagans proposed a toast with Champagne, and they crossed arms to take a sip.

I believe that the meals served at the White House State Dinners not only *could* have a profound effect on the meetings conducted by the Presidents, but *do* have a profound effect.

Nancy Reagan was an elegant First Lady, and she made it her job to keep Mrs. Gorbachev happy. Whenever she spoke and the translators translated Nancy's words, Mrs. Gorbachev would always smile. These are the things that are the most noticeable to chefs serving food at the White House. Nancy Reagan was a master at making sure her guests were enjoying themselves.

Ronald Reagan and Nancy Reagan worked together as a team making sure that everything was the epitome of perfection. For instance, all the chefs serving the food would hold their trays exactly the same, and then place them on the food stands in complete unison. It was a beautiful sight, and the Gorbachev's had never seen anything like it.

Mikhail Gorbachev and Ronald Reagan remained friends after both were out of office, and I believe the treatment that President Reagan gave him when he was here was one of the things that eased the pressures of the Cold War until the Berlin Wall was taken down at President Reagan's request in 1989. It may be fantasy, but this is what I believe.

One of the ways you knew President Reagan was fond of someone was because he would tease them. He loved to talk about Gorbachev's famous birthmark, which was a long purple mark running from his hair down to his forehead. President Reagan told him it looked like a country on a map.

"It is a sign of intelligence and a great leader." Mr. Gorbachev replied.

Mikhail Gorbachev was my favorite foreign dignitary, He wasn't a hard nose, and abrasive or arrogant. He always thanked us for the work we did.

CHAPTER FIVE
The Kitchen Brigade

When I first arrived on the scene and took my position on the kitchen staff, I didn't have any idea how things worked at the White House. I learned quickly that the White House kitchen staffs 250 employees. They work after the pattern of the French culinary brigades in Paris that have been structured for centuries.

Cook 3 - Cleans and prepares vegetables.

Cook 2 - Begins a cooking career under a Level 3 Chef.

Cook 1 - Prepares pastries under a Level 2 Chef.

Chef Level 3 - Works and learns under Level 2 Chef.

Chef Level 2 - Makes pastries.

Chef Level 1 - Works under the Sous Chef.

Sous Chef - Makes the salads and presents desserts, controls the garde manger.

Executive Sous Chef - Manages the Kitchen and cooks the entrée.

Executive Chef - The Head Supervisor – He is responsible for time sheets, creates the recipes, creates the menus, purchases the food, and is in charge of production costs.

Master Chef - Is not responsible to cook. He is the ultimate supervisor who tastes the food, creates the design presentations, hires and fires anyone on the spot if need be. He is the Sanitation Supervisor and is one-to-one with the Vice President of the United States in Kitchen 2.

Executive Master Chef Kitchen 1 - He is the most powerful chef in the White House and is one-to-one with the President of the United States.

I had to learn these things quickly and made it my business to know my way around the entire process. I was watched very closely because of constant questions but never made myself obnoxious. I was a short brown man learning and bent on making this chef business in the White House work for me.

One of the things that intrigued me was how friendly the Secret Service was with the kitchen staff.

We interacted with them all the time. They were on the run all the time and didn't have a lot of time to eat, so they would run into the kitchen, and we would cook for them. We made special meals that they could eat quickly, digest without getting gas, and ginger ale was the drink of the day. Ginger ale keeps you from farting because it helps digest your food really fast. No matter how much they begged, we never gave them too much gassy food. We never, ever fed them beans. They loved our casseroles with lots of barbecued meat, but we wouldn't put any barbecue sauce on any of it.

The habit of the Secret Service was to call ahead and tell the Head Chef that they had forty-five minutes to eat. One of the main reasons the Secret Service was so endeared to the kitchen was because food would be waiting on them when they got there. Tables would be set with silverware, plates, and drinks, and the food would be coming. They never had to wait a minute on their food, and they had time to sit and eat instead of eating on the run like they would if the food preparation was late.

The White House has three kitchens, and all have a different set of staff at different levels of cooking experience. There are 64 chefs in the kitchens. All the staffs are certified chefs no matter what their particular jobs were. I started in Kitchen 3 that had a staff of 40 chefs. Kitchen 2 staffs 18 chefs, and Kitchen 1 only six.

The chefs in the White House are no strangers to hard work and long hours. For instance, the supervisors arrive at 3:00 a.m. before the regular chefs who come at 5:00 a.m. The supervisors meet from 3:00 a.m. to 5:00 a.m.

Before I was in the supervisory position, I was known for being early at everything I did. I would always arrive at exactly 4:30 a.m., and I would start work as soon as I got there. I was bent on making a clear understanding that I wasn't there to play around but was dedicated to serving the Presidents of the United States. All the chefs took their jobs seriously, but no chef was more dedicated than I was.

Supervisors work most nights until 9:00 p.m. The head supervisor works until 10:00 p.m., and still has to be back to work at 3:00 a.m. He is responsible for walking through the facilities and making sure everything is in its place. He makes sure all the staff is there, and makes sure everybody understands what the day's production will be. The head supervisor takes nobody's word for anything. He verifies the system himself because he has the ultimate responsibility if things go wrong.

If the supervisor finds something wrong or out of place, he will call the chef responsible and tell him to get to work a hour early and fix it. That discipline has a tendency to keep everybody on his toes, and makes the White House kitchens similar to the military in their standards of operation.

Most of the chefs work five days in the week, but many of those days are twenty hours. Sometimes the public gets the wrong idea about the kitchen and thinks the kitchens are open twenty-four hours, but they aren't. They are open seven days, but the chefs take turns being on call for those days. They supply a morning crew that works until lunch and is responsible for lunch. Another crew arrives at lunch and works to the evening dinner. There is a crew coming for dinner, and the two cross over preparing the evening meal, so the system is a science just as their cooking is.

The White House chefs have a ranking system that is quite sophisticated called "The Brigade."

I started my career under President Ronald Reagan as a regular chef. In this system there are chefs of different distinctions, and they are given the jobs that they have the most expertise doing.

The jobs include Sauté Chef, Soup Chef, Pastry Chef, and the Garde Manger. The Garde Manger Chef's job is to watch over the foods that needs to be kept cool or in refrigeration.

The Grill Chefs are next followed in rank by the Sous Chefs. Next up the ladder is the Executive Sous Chef, the Executive Chef, and then finally the Master Chef.

The Master Chef is the top of the line, and this is the position every chef that enters the White House kitchen hopes to attain. It is the most coveted position in the industry of making food.

I started out my career serving President Reagan in the Number 3 kitchen with the rank of chef. I was at the bottom – you couldn't even go down from there.

I was introduced to the rugged routine of a junior chef working in Kitchen 3. I began work at 5:30 a.m., and my job was to take care of the vegetables. I was in charge of cleaning, prepping, and cutting them up, but I was not allowed to cook the vegetables. I had not arrived at that level yet.

I cut up and prepared more vegetables than I care to remember. I did not use machinery. I had my prized collection of knives.

I kept the knives at peak performance by sharpening them every day. I was not a novice because I worked at the lower level in the kitchen; I had already honed my skills cutting up and preparing vegetables for salads because I was a school trained chef.

I mainly honed my skills by watching and learning from the other chefs I worked under. When it was time to go home, I would hang around, and the other chefs would let me "practice."

The one thing that I did learn was that I was no way near an Executive Chef.

I stayed after hours to learn. I was hungry to pick up every thing I possibly could learn from the chefs. I read hundreds and hundreds of cookbooks of every sort you can imagine. After all of the energy and effort I had put into my work as a level 3 cook in Kitchen 3, I was promoted up to level 1.

CHAPTER SIX
The First Lady

As everyone will learn while reading this book, the First Ladies of the White House have everything in the world to do with
who cooks in the kitchens. When I came on board, I was told
while they were processing me that I needed to get up to the
White House and meet with Nancy Reagan.

I was given a pass and nervously headed to Mrs. Reagan's
office. When I got there, I had a wait that lasted about thirty minutes, and then the Chief of Staff called me to come into the First
Lady's eloquent office.

I was stunned at the beauty this elderly lady attained. She
was dressed to the nines in the middle of a workday, and those
famous pearls hung so smartly around her neck. She was thin
and obviously in good shape, and she smiled like someone out of
Hollywood – well – because she was out of Hollywood, and she
married a very famous actor, who became the Governor of California for eight years and now President of the United States.

This new chef on the block did not know what to expect because it was unusual for a lowly one tier chef to be standing in
front of a lady who could deny his existence and wipe him off the
roster of the White House kitchen staff.

"I've heard so much about you, Chef Seaton," she said with
no hesitation. "All my husband talks about when he mentions
the kitchens is a young man by the name of Ronnie Seaton, who
can really cook. Please sit for a moment."

The only word that can adequately describe Nancy Reagan

is "eloquent" because she was in every sense of the word. Her mannerisms were perfect, and she could make you feel like nobody else existed on the planet at that moment.

I felt an emotion that I would feel over and over throughout my service to the President and First Lady.

She began her conversation by filling me in on all the things she liked to eat, and then she filled out her conversation by making sure that I understood about all the things President Reagan like to eat.

I worked in Kitchen 3. There were a lot of chefs in Kitchen 3, and they cooked for the State Department. What was I doing here?

"I know I'm not going to be cooking for you, Mrs. Reagan." I said while forcing down the jitters in my voice.

"Okay," Mrs. Reagan said. "But be aware that at any time we might request that you prepare a special meal for us."

The thought thrilled me, so I told the First Lady that I would look forward to cooking any meal the President and the First Lady wanted.

"You know I am a stickler for detail," Mrs. Reagan added.

"Madam First Lady," I replied respectfully, "I have been in the military and was a drill Sergeant at one time, so I know about details."

"You are going to work out just fine. If my husband thought enough of you to bring you all the way from New Orleans to the White House, then you must be okay."

I said goodbye to the First Lady, and that was the last time I saw her for a while, and then one day Mrs. Reagan sent a request to Kitchen 3 to dismiss me, so that she could talk to me.

Mrs. Reagan was having a function, and she selected me to come and help with it. It was then that I found out how tough Nancy Reagan was. In fact, I have said many times when describing her that she should have been a drill Sergeant.

Nancy entered the room where the chefs were preparing for the event, and then with no warning she shouted to the head Steward: "You better make sure that everything you're doing is absolutely perfect, or you won't be the head Steward; you'll be the headless Steward and out of here tomorrow!"

She let the whole place know she meant business and not to mess with her, so nobody did. All the workers began hopping and jumping like nobody's business making sure they weren't in the line of fire as this feisty little lady took total charge of her territory.

Mrs. Reagan pulled a 6-inch ruler and pieces of string from her pocket. The strings were of different lengths, so that she knew exactly the measure of certain items on the table. The ruler was used for items that were to be exactly 6 inches in length or apart.

Everything had to be identical on the table with zero tolerance for variations. Two plates could not be different distances from the silverware for instance. She took a couple of measures, and then ordered that everything be off the table in five minutes and reset to the new standards. No one expected a reaction like this from such a small and somewhat frail lady.

Mrs. Reagan found a wrinkle in one of the tablecloths, so she forced the chefs to re-iron every tablecloth so that they were all smooth and beautiful. All the chefs including myself understood in one meeting with this First Lady that there would be no nonsense, and that she would demand this kind of attention to detail so get used to it.

She said sternly to those at attention, "If you can't do this, then I will find somebody that can."

She walked up to me and bluntly asked me, "Would you like to be a Supervisor?"

"With all due respect First Lady," I replied. "I don't think I want to do that. I am in the line of fire and will make enemies because I am so new."

"I'm in charge here," Nancy Reagan commented. "Nobody's going to bully you around as long as I'm in charge."

I was on my toes in the matter, so I answered her matter-of-factly. "With all due respect First Lady, I can't take your offer. I have a lot to learn, and I don't want to fail you. Please let me have some more time to learn how things work around here and if at the appropriate time if you still feel the way you do now, I'll accept your offer."

Nancy Reagan actually smiled while looking at this innocent person who may have been a novice as a chef, but was not a novice as a human being.

"At least you're honest with me, and I respect that." She said softly.

That was the first introduction I had as to how Nancy Reagan was going to run the show. I understood perfectly where she was coming from. I believed and bought into her reasoning when some of the others were complaining about her standards being ridiculously high.

I had the idea that this country had set high standards throughout the world and if you are the President and First Lady, then you were expected to make sure those same standards were shown whether you were meeting an important head of state, or you were sitting down to a lovely dinner. Nancy Reagan set the bar high, and those who couldn't measure up weren't around very long.

Nancy Reagan demonstrated her intolerance of playing around with her expectations. Before one event, she picked up a plate of food and threw it on the floor. She said the food and preparation was not up to the level of what the President of the United States should expect. It took less than twenty minutes for Mrs. Reagan to terminate that chef.

The entire brigade of kitchen staff found out that this Lady in charge was not going to play around. She did set high standards, but all she asked was that the kitchen staff abide by the rules whether they agreed with them or not.

Nancy Reagan was also just. She was very compassionate, caring, and a person with extremely high values and morals.

There wasn't a mean bone in her body, and I think the reason she and I got along so well was because I had set those same standards for myself. We liked each other, and I lasted long because she recognized those same values in me.

I had no problem with authority. I understood the chain of command, and I knew who my bosses were. The President, the Vice President, the First Lady, the Vice President's wife, the Cabinet members, and the higher ranked chefs were my bosses, and I understood that fact better than anyone around I worked under.

Honestly, I only had one thing on my mind, and that was to become the best chef I could possibly be. I had no aspirations to upstage another chef or disrespect them by trying to do better than all those around me. I simply wanted to master and hone the skills of my job. I wanted to be the best that I could be. I studied and studied. Every time there was a class I could attend in which I could better myself, I enrolled in that class. Professional development was at the top of my list, and I attended many courses in Culinary Arts the entire time I was a chef.

If I were going to please a little roaring lioness like Nancy Reagan, I had to get up to that level. I understood that.

I have described her like this: "She was a great First Lady, she really was. She was tough, and many people didn't understand how such a little bitty lady could roar like a lioness. It was good times with her and bad times with her. But you know, it was hard to see her and President Reagan leave. I was sad for a long time."

CHAPTER SEVEN
Out of the Ordinary Reflections

It is very unusual for a chef who is working in a lower kitchen to have access at any time to the President of the United States, but Ronald Reagan kept his promise and never forgot me.

The President would call at times down to Kitchen 3 and ask the head chef to allow me to do some private little things for him. There was no stopping this and no interferences. When the President called and made a request, he meant for the request to be granted, no one was foolish enough to stand in the way.

When the President called for me to report, I reported. It didn't make any difference what I was doing.

A problem may seem to arise in the kitchen as to some being envious of a junior chef getting presidential attention, but it was never a problem. White House chefs are professionals, so the chefs were proud that a President would call one of their own to duty. It was an honor that someone from their kitchen would represent them. It brought special attention to them.

The White House kitchens are as sanitary as a hospital. The whole staff works hard to keep them that way. In one situation, the Steward was sick, and there was no one to clean the bathroom, so I made sure that the bathroom was clean because I cleaned it. There many occasions that arose when the chefs had to make sure our entire work area was sanitary. I would never eat in a restaurant if the bathroom was not clean.

I learned the manners and standards that all chefs and cooks working in American restaurants and serving the public should adhere to. President Reagan was the cleanest man I ever met. I couldn't meet him with bacteria all over me. I would never enter the presence of the President with a soiled jacket. I don't wipe my hands on my apron; I wash my hands with soap and dry on a clean towel. My hair was clean and cut, my nails were clean, I had no sleep in my eyes, and my breath never smelled. I couldn't carry germs into the presence of the President of the United States.

I never left the practice of being immaculately clean. I believe that every cook no matter where he serves should have the same manners with the public as if he were serving the President of the United States.

I never wore cologne either. We weren't allowed to wear cologne in culinary school because the smell of cologne will change the taste of the food in your mouth.

Nancy Reagan would not allow any hint of unsanitary conditions anywhere in the White House. She would not allow facial hair on the staff. She started that ban because she was protecting in her own way the President of the highest office in the world.

All the Presidents had a dog except the Clinton's. One afternoon, President Reagan's dog got loose and ended up in the kitchen. The chefs were running all over the place trying to catch the dog when suddenly he jumped on the table where two filet mignon steaks were marinating that the President and First Lady would have that night for dinner.

The dog ate one of the steaks, and the Executive Chef was trying to pull his hair out. Those steaks were specially flown in, so this was the recipe for disaster. Finally, one of the chefs said,

"We have other steaks. The President won't know the difference."

I was standing nearby and heard the remark. "There is no way that is going to happen," I said rather sternly. They weren't used to me being so assertive, but I meant business, and they knew it.

The steaks were tender, so the dog had no problem woofing it down in a gulp or two before anything could be done about it. So what were they to do?

The Head Chef got on the phone and started calling hotels all over Washington explaining the dilemma at the White House. He finally found an Italian restaurant that was using the same meat supplier, so the Secret Service and the chef got in a car and took off to retrieve it.

It wasn't long before the Secret Service and the chef arrived with the metal box containing dry ice, so the steaks wouldn't change colors, and the day was saved. The hardest part was cleaning and sanitizing where the dog had slobbered saliva all over the prep table. Once we got that done, the dog peed on the floor. Afterwards, we laughed about that incident for years, and I don't think President Reagan or the First Lady ever found out about it.

The Reagan's had several dogs, and this one was a big black Bouvier des Flandres. The dog's name was Lucky, and he got lucky that night.

"The dog meant no harm," I explained to a younger chef, who thought the dog should the euthenized. "Someone forgot to feed him and when he smelled food, he took off and found it. He was hungry, that's all."

President Reagan wasn't afraid to mix it up with the families that worked in the White House no matter at what level. One Easter, the White House was having an Easter egg hunt for all the children of the Cabinet Members.

These kids weren't from poor families, so they were dressed in their Sunday best clothes. The girls had on their Easter chiffon dresses, and the boys were dressed in sport coats and ties.

A couple of chefs and their kids were invited including my family because they were serving food on the lawn, and we were allowed to bring our kids. The children were having a great time.

The kids started clamoring and pointing to something totally unexpected. The President and First Lady were on the lawn coming toward the Easter egg hunt. Both were dressed as immaculately as if they were walking down the aisle of a church.

It is a White House tradition at the Easter egg hunts every year that the kids push the eggs and roll them across the lawn.

The President was determined to be a kid again, so he started pushing the eggs.

The dog had been let loose on the lawn and had pooped on it. The President stepped in it, slipped and fell in the poop, and then started laughing. All the kids were dying laughing because it was so hilarious to see the President of the United States all dressed up and lying in dog poop. Well, Mrs. Reagan wasn't so thrilled. She banned that dog from ever stepping foot on the White House lawn again.

Ronald Reagan was that kind of President. He was always dressed up, but he was never a "stuffed shirt," and people adored him. I have said many times through the years that I never met anyone who knew Ronald Reagan that didn't love him.

The presidential dog was always getting into trouble. The President is most often transported to the airport and other places nearby in the presidential helicopter. President Reagan was often seen holding the leash and trailing a dog that was nearly pulling him off balance.

The President was taking a trip in Air Force One, so the helicopter landed in its normal spot on the lawn. President Reagan and the First Lady came walking out of the house, and the President was trailing the dog holding the leash. Suddenly, the dog lunged and caused the collar to slip the over the dog's head and left the President holding an empty leash.

The Secret Service attending to the President started chasing the dog, but the dog was much faster than those guys. The dog was darting all over the place with no one able to stop him, and he was very fast.

The President seemed amused while watching this spectacle, and then he decided to end the melee. He put two fingers between his lips and *shssshsshsst* he blew a loud shrilling whistle. The dog's ears perked up, and he came to a complete halt, while several of the Secret Service men were laying on the ground. Mr. Reagan said later that he'd seen enough bull crap and put a stop to it before his servicemen embarrassed themselves any further.

The President whistled again, and the dog made a beeline

straight towards him. The President had total control of that dog. The dog's name was Rex, and he was the favorite dog in the White House. Many people said the dog could understand every word spoken to him. Mrs. Reagan told the dog to never run off again, and the dog never did.

I worked with five presidents, but I loved Ronald Reagan the most. This is how I described the President in a recent interview:

"He was the greatest spokesman of all the Presidents. He didn't need a teleprompter most of the time until his Alzheimer problems began. He loved his wife. He loved his children. He loved his country, and he loved horses. He will be remembered someday as the greatest President of them all."

I was apprehensive when I came on board with a white Republican boss. After all, the White House was a hodgepodge of political activity. I had no idea how I would fare working in that kind of environment. I was a Democrat, but the President didn't see me as a boy or a man. He didn't see me as an Afro-American. He treated me as an American, who served his country, loved his family, was a devout Catholic, and had strong deep morals and values

I confess that if Ronald Reagan suddenly appeared and asked me to do it all over again, I would sign on with the President in a heartbeat and wouldn't even pray about it.

President Reagan said to me when it came time for his final term to end: "Chef, you love God, and I know He comes first in your life. You are a strong family man, and you love your President."

CHAPTER EIGHT
The First Families

One of the delights of being a chef in the White House is you get to know the First Family children and become friends and mentors to them.

President Reagan kept his family out of the limelight. Only Nancy was in the public eye a lot of the time. The President loved holidays, and Christmas was the biggest day in the house of the President. He would come and visit the families of the White House staff including the kitchen staff. He and Mrs. Reagan would bring gifts to our family and he would tell us how much he appreciated us because he was a lover of his family; even though, to the public he sometimes may have seemed distant. He really was involved in their lives at least at the White House.

Michael Reagan, the adopted son of Ronald Reagan, visited the White House often, and I liked him for being the most articulate of the grown children of President Reagan. There aren't many significant stories about the Reagan family, but the children of the Presidents who did live in the house were for the most part respectful.

President Reagan loved a certain cookie that I made when he was in Kitchen 3. One certain day, my cookies didn't come out like they were supposed to bake. The Head Chef wouldn't let the cookies go up to the President.

"Where are Chef's cookies?" the President asked.

My cookies had crumbled because I didn't have enough butter in them, and the President was informed of this.

"No, no," he said, "I want to see the cookies so send Chef Ronnie up here."

No one knew for certain why the President was so adamant about this, but I headed up to the Oval Office with what I had. The President tasted the cookies.

"They're good, Chef, but they're breaking all up," the President commented while crumbs were dropping all over his desk and brown suit.

The kids came in the office. They saw the cookies and told the President that they didn't care if they were broken; they would eat them.

Later in the day, a note came down to the kitchen from the President ordering me to make some more cookies but make sure they're done right. I made five-dozen cookies, and they came out perfect.

It took two days to make the cookies and when they were put into a box, the Secret Service wouldn't let me go up to the Oval Office because there were some dignitaries in that the President wanted to keep private.

The cookies lasted only two days because the kids tore into them. They were oatmeal raisin cookies made with real California raisins. Those cookies became a staple in the White House during the entire tenure of President Ronald Reagan.

There was no bickering in the White House among the Reagan family. Nancy didn't allow any heavy drinking or wild parties. She was very strict, and she set some very high standards.

President Reagan did not curse when anyone was around, and he and Nancy never fought in public. You would never know they ever had a cross word with each other.

Nancy was the only one of the two who would raise her voice. She only did this when she gave a directive that wasn't followed although the kids did mostly what they wanted as long as they weren't in the way. They did very well in school as did the children of Ronald Reagan from his previous marriage to Jane Wyman.

One of the main sources of gossip was the Secret Service.

They know a lot about what is going on all over the place, and they never once mentioned to me that they had to take stuff from the Reagan's, and there was never any slamming or breaking stuff. That was not true of the behavior with other Presidents.

CHAPTER NINE
The Vice President

Only twice in the history of our country has a Vice President been elected President – Richard Nixon and George Bush, Sr. Only Richard Nixon won re-election of the office. President Nixon did not succeed his Vice Presidential office under President Dwight D. Eisenhower. Nixon won the election in a landslide eight years later after losing to President John F. Kennedy in 1960.

I did not work in Kitchen 2 during the George Bush, Sr. term of office. Kitchen 2 is the kitchen that handles food for the Vice President and Cabinet. The times that I got involved with the Vice President was when there was a late night food order coming down, and that only happened a couple of times.

One of those times was when the President was working late dealing with Russia on the Berlin Wall situation. I got selected to prepare the food for the late night work session. I took the food up to the meeting, and that's the first time I actually saw Vice President Bush face-to-face. I was immediately struck by the commanding presence of George Bush, Sr.

"He looked important and presidential," I explained to my wife, Annie, while barely containing my excitement at finally seeing the Vice President. "I didn't get to talk to him because you just don't walk up to somebody that important and start a conversation."

I got to meet Barbara Bush. Mrs. Bush was a super woman. She is right at the top of the list of my favorite Vice Presidential wives or First Ladies that I served.

I loved the Bush family, and it was a large extended family that came to the White House often. I met George W. Bush, Jr. and Jeb Bush, and I respected them. Vice President Bush was so proud of his boys, and no one knew at the time that George W. Bush would become President of the United States or his brother would one day run for the office.

Vice President Bush was President Reagan's right hand man and his best friend. He was a negotiator, and he knew when to step in and calm things down. The consensus with everyone working with Vice President Bush was he was a gentleman and took his job as serious as any Vice President that served his country.

George H. Bush never raised his voice, and he didn't curse very much unlike President Reagan, who didn't curse at all. When Vice President Bush was upset, he would slam his fist on the table to make a point. He was respected as a very intelligent man but had a humility about him that was uncanny for a man of this power.

Barbara Bush was known around the White House as being very honest, and she always told the truth. You knew where she stood, and she never played around with your emotions. That is not true of every lady I worked with at the highest offices of the United States.

She was in total charge of her kids. She did let them play around the White House. They loved to play hide-and-seek. Sometimes they were playing around the place, and one of them would come down to the kitchens to hide. It wouldn't be long before one of them would find the other, and the game would end because they got interested in what was being cooked in the kitchen.

One day I was running up from Kitchen 3 where I was working while George Bush, Sr. was the Vice President. I was taking something up to Kitchen 2, and the kids were in the kitchen requesting fried peanut butter sandwiches. They wanted me to try one, so I did, and it was good. The kids also liked hamburgers, so they would get out of the way of their mom and run to one of the kitchens to get a burger and French fries.

Those days in the White House starting out were some of the happiest times of my life. I enjoyed working there, and I never thought I would be moving on to work with another President. I thought, as I saw the movement of chefs when a new regime took over, that I would move on out of the White House and end up working as a chef in a hotel or restaurant somewhere like all the other career chefs, but that wasn't to be.

CHAPTER TEN
President Ronald Reagan's Favorite Meals
How He Liked to Dress

Breakfast

2 eggs sunny side up

1 strip of bacon

1 slice of wheat bread toasted, cut in half diagonally, buttered, and strawberry preserves

1 glass of freshly squeezed orange juice with the pulp removed

1 cup of Columbian coffee made black

Lunch

President Reagan did not eat lunch.

Reagan loved oatmeal cookies – exactly 4 inches in diameter, brown sugar, golden raisins (he didn't like black raisins because he thought they looked like bugs), and walnuts from California.

Fast Foods

President Reagan did not eat fast foods from any restaurant.

Favorite Alcoholic Beverage

President Reagan did not drink alcohol except an occasional sip of Champagne at special functions.

How He Dressed

President Reagan wore a suit and tie every day to work. He loved wearing and made famous the brown suit.

★ ★ ★ ★ ★

REAGAN

•

ICEBERG LETTUCE

with garlic croutons, roasted cherry tomatoes,
and crispy crumbled bacon,
all topped with a creamy blue cheese dressing

SEARED NEW YORK STRIP

glazed in a balsamic demi-gloss,
twice-baked potato with sour cream, pepper jack cheese,
and bacon bits, with a side of fresh seasoned cauliflower

LATTICE TOPPED APPLE PIE A-LA-MODE

with vanilla ice-cream –
made with fresh Granny Smith apples

———— • ————

PREPARATIONS FOR TWO PEOPLE

SALAD

2 iceberg lettuce wedges,
4 oz creamy bleu cheese dressing
2 oz roasted cherry tomatoes
2 oz crumbled bacon
Garlic croutons
Prep – Mix salad with ingredients, toss and serve

ENTRÉE

8 oz New York Strip (2)
¼ cup balsamic demi-gloss
2 large russet potatoes
¼ cup sour cream
¼ cup heavy whipping cream
8 tbsp unsalted butter
½ cup pepper jack cheese
½ cup bacon bits
Salt and pepper (to taste)
4 oz cauliflower (cut in quarters)

DIRECTIONS

1) Season steak strip w/ kosher salt and white pepper, leave dry rub to marinate until room temp.

2) Sear both sides and all edges in cast-iron skillet, place in oven at 425 degrees for eight minutes until cooked to medium rare, or has an internal temp of 150 degrees.

3) Wash large russet potatoes and pat dry, place on sheet pan in oven at 375 degrees for 40 minutes. Remove from oven and slice open. Scoop out potato and add sour cream, heavy cream, butter, pepper jack cheese, and

bacon bits (add salt and pepper to taste). Put potato back into peel and bake 5 minutes to melt cheese.

4) Slice cauliflower into quarters, place in mesh basket above boiling salt water pot, season w/ unsalted butter, kosher salt and white pepper.

5) Combine all on plate and serve.

DESSERT

4 GRANNY SMITH apples (peeled, cored, and sliced – place in lemon juice* to avoid browning)

2 cups brown sugar

½ stick unsalted butter

1 tbsp cinnamon

1 tsp nutmeg

1 tbsp pure vanilla

½ cup apple juice

DIRECTIONS

1) Bake pie crust seven minutes at 350 degrees.

2) Mix all ingredients (apple slices, brown sugar, butter, cinnamon, nutmeg, vanilla, apple juice) in pot on medium heat. Cook until melted. Remove apples and pat dry. Place apples at bottom of pie crust shell, pour sauce over.

3) Cut strips from second pie shell and place across top.

4) Wrap aluminum foil around edge of pie (to avoid burning).

5) Bake pie at 350 degrees for 50 min.

6) Let cool.

7) Serve.

*Any acidic juice will do to prevent browning.

SECTION 2
PRESIDENT GEORGE H. W. BUSH

CHAPTER ONE
Getting Started

I stressed a lot about what would happen to me when President Reagan's term of office was finished. I had many sleepless nights trying to figure out how I could manipulate the system and stay on board.

I was counting on the fact that I already had the connection with President Bush when he was the Vice President that might bode well when the Bush's were settling on their culinary staff. I could be left in the kitchen or booted out.

It wasn't long after the new President came on board that the Executive Chef of Kitchen 3 called us all together for a meeting.

"There will be some changes," he explained. "Some of you or all of you including me could be terminated tomorrow when we go up to meet the President and Mrs. Bush."

It was impossible to feel good about this, so my stomach churned again. I was getting prepared, so I told myself that this was a nice visit, and a great experience not too many people will ever have. I had resigned to the fact that I was too low on the totem pole to remain in the kitchen. We went up to meet with President and Mrs. Bush. Our entire staff was standing and talking with them. Things settled down, and it was time for the roll call to see who would remain, and who would go.

To my surprise my name was called. I was going to stay, and I was so thrilled I wanted to shout but out of respect for the others, I restrained myself from any outburst of emotion.

Not only did my name get called that I would not be let go, but I was informed that I would be moving up in rank in Kitchen 3. At the snap of a finger, I moved up from Prep Chef to Cooking Chef, and I would be preparing the whole meal for the State Department. I was the only African American who stayed and worked for President Bush, Sr. No one else was promoted, and most of the Kitchen 3 staff were let go.

President Bush walked over to me and said it was his personal invitation that I stay on if I wanted to continue.

"Thank you, Mr. President," I said.

Mrs. Bush came over and called me by my first name. "Ronnie, we're proud to have you on our staff."

"Thank you, Mrs. Bush. I will work hard if not harder than I already have, and I hope to please you in everything I do."

I got the promotion and started a new gig. I was in charge of the meals for the department heads, and their meals were very diverse and complicated. I had to learn to cook special diets and for those who had allergies to certain food. My culinary skills were put to the ultimate test, and it was difficult and going to get more so.

I had an entire staff of white people, and it was hard at first because they didn't want to accept me as their supervisor. I asked for a meeting. I told them that I was just like them. I was in Vietnam, and I didn't see skin color. I bagged the bodies of white boys, black boys, yellow boys, and the only color I saw was red.

Then I asked them if I could pray. One chef was an atheist and tried to shut us down, but I prevailed, and we prayed. As a matter of fact, we prayed everyday before we started work, and the chefs appreciated it so much. The kitchen staff finally realized what my moral values were, and what I was all about.

I started traditions to win the crew over. For a long time, not one of them called in sick or asked for extended time off. We were a team. We had picnics for the families, and celebrated every one's birthday and had a party. It was great.

I got promoted to Executive Chef of Kitchen 3. I was in my league and happy out of this world. I made many changes and brought more elaborate meals than the State Department ever had before. I made lobster dishes, foie gras which is a sautéed duck recipe, duck under glass with an orange glaze, and many more exotic types of food that made me a hero with those guys from the State Department.

Food in my kitchen was like eating at Piccadilly's but on a high end restaurant scale. There was no price for anyone who was permitted to eat in the kitchen, and that was primarily the entire State Department. You swiped your clearance card and then ordered your food. It had to be quick because they only had forty-five minutes to eat. It was much easier to eat there than to go into the city, and then have to go through all the clearances to get back into the White House.

I went above and beyond what was necessary to keep everybody satisfied, and they appreciated it President Bush came to Kitchen 3 now and then to eat because of the food we were serving. Whenever he found out I was making clam chowder, he'd be down there because he loved my clam chowder.

One of President Bush's favorite meals I made that he would come down for was white chili. The chili is made with white Navy beans, roasted chicken, jalapeños, cilantro, heavy cream with a roux, white wine, and French butter. We made a delicious pita bread that was cut in triangles, so he could eat it with the chili. He loved this chili almost as good as anything I would make for him.

We knew the daddy was coming when it was White Chili Day. He also loved steaks, so I would order filet mignon for him and put it on the menu calendar for the month, so he would know when to come down for a great steak.

I really got to know President Bush because of all the trips he made down to Kitchen 3 to eat my food. I didn't cook for him personally, so this was the way to his heart. He would bring everybody down there. The Vice President, Dan Quale, would come down there with the President.

My crew stopped me one day and said, "Ronnie you have to stop doing this."

"Stop doing it?" I answered. "He's got too many people coming down here."

It got to the point where some of the dignitaries visiting the White House heard about the food in Kitchen 3 would come down there. It was a nice place, and I made sure we kept it that way. Everything was perfect down to the chairs in a perfect row. Thanks to First Lady Nancy Reagan, we had learned how to keep it all in proportion. Mrs. Reagan would come down there and inspect. Mrs. Bush would come down there to give us a hug.

During President Ronald Reagan's second term of office, I got to spend more time getting to know Vice President Bush. The President had a lot of barbecues, and I was always invited as one of the chefs to prepare some of the food. I learned his mannerisms and at the end of his term as Vice President, we knew he would be running for office as President of the United States, but I had no idea I would be working for him.

George H. Bush won the office, and Barbara Bush decided that I was going to remain in the White House. She asked me to move up to Kitchen 2, but I told her that I hadn't learned enough yet, so I stayed in Kitchen 3.

President Bush had a different relationship with his wife as First Lady than President Reagan did with Nancy. The Bush's sort of ran things together, and I loved Barbara Bush because she was the most caring person I ever worked with.

President Bush was a simplistic man. He was plain and didn't show much of an extravagancy you might expect in the President of the United States. For instance, the favorite snack on his desk was beef jerky. He loved the sweet kind that had a teriyaki glaze, and you would often see him chewing on a piece while he was relaxing or working in the Oval Office. We made the beef jerky in the kitchen.

The President was a meat and potatoes kind of guy. He loved meatloaf. What was so funny was Mrs. Bush would come down to the kitchen and show us how to make food for her husband. We would come up from Kitchen 3 to Kitchen 2 to watch how she wanted things made, so that when we were called upon to make clam chowder or something her husband was used to eating, we would know the exact recipe.

She wanted certain food made with margarine instead of butter. When she first came in and started showing us how to make stuff, we accommodated her. She made garlic mashed potatoes with margarine. The first time she was in the kitchen and started inquiring about where the margarine was, the Head Chef said,

"Oh, Mrs. Bush we don't cook with margarine down here."

"Well in my house we do. I have too many kids."

She was serious about this. It was the sense of saving the tax payers money, and that is why there was an innocence about her that made you love her. Neither of them were extravagant in any way, shape, or form.

We made pies. Lots and lots of pies. The Bush's loved sweet potato pies, pumpkin pies, and apple pies. We made these all the time and especially during the holidays. We made brownies and cookies, but the most unusual request Mrs. Bush had was for candy. We bought no candy; we made all the candy in the kitchen. The kids loved Rice Krispie treats with M&M'S inside.

We made delicious candied apples on a stick, and everybody loved Halloween because of the many varieties of candy made in the kitchen.

Mrs. Bush loved to throw parties. The lady believed in a birthday party for everybody. When your child was born, she would come to the hospital and bring gifts and guess who showed up, too? That's right President Bush would come to the hospital when one of the staff wives had a baby. They were wonderful people.

President Bush was a pizza eater. He loved his pizzas. He would come up with these concoctions like lobster on pizza, and ask us to make one or two for him. We made them with crab, shrimp, Italian sausage, and anchovies. He insisted that every pizza was made with olive oil, and he didn't want cheese on the pizza but layer it with portabella mushrooms, jalapenos, black olives, and red sliced onions.

President Bush was a worldly man meaning he knew about

life. He was a former FBI Director before his political career. He was a family man, and he taught me a lot about how to raise my kids.

"Never whip your children," he said to me. "Sit down and talk to them. Reason with them as to why they're being punished. Tell them how important it is to learn never to do it again."

Mrs. Bush is the one who told me to play classical music to your child before he or she is born.

"Play Mozart and other famous musicians," she said. "Your child will build brain cells and when the child is born, he will already be starting to think."

I did this with all my children before they were born and judging by the way my children turned out, there is something to this rather strange philosophy.

I loved cooking for the Bush's because it was a beautiful thing. They would have a gathering of the children at some of the meals. President and Mrs. Bush loved their children and anybody's children. They loved having kids around them and delighted in the camaraderie and joy they found in their family. Mrs. Bush loved her sons, daughters-in-law, and her grand children. Both of the Bush's loved people, and it was always evident in their demeanor in the presence of company no matter who it was visiting them.

When the President and First Lady Bush came to the White House, it was like having your grandparents there. When Mrs. Bush visited Kitchen 3, I thought she would tell me goodbye. Instead, she found out that President Reagan brought me to the White House. She came to me and gave me a big ole kiss and a bear hug.

The crew began to buzz and finally asked me if that was a goodbye hug or what? The First Lady asked me if I was ready to move up in rank to the next kitchen. It was at that time I told her again that I needed to learn more and when I was ready, I would contact her.

I finally did move up to Kitchen 2 at the last of their term. When that happened, I really got to cook for them and the Cabinet. Those were some of the best times of my whole life because the Bush's were so nurturing. There was nothing we could ask them they wouldn't do.

Back then, the schools had "Report Card" day. Parents would go to the school when it was time to pass out the report cards. The President never refused to let us go to Report Card Day at our children's schools. Mrs. Bush asked us to give her a paper stating when each child was getting their report cards, and she made sure that we had all the time we needed to visit our children's schools.

President George Bush, Sr. believed that God should come first, then your family. Annie and I were having children quickly and on our way to eight kids. When I needed to take off to attend to the needs of the family, President Bush never stood in the way, so we loved him and appreciated him so much.

CHAPTER TWO
On My Way to Kitchen 2

There were only three occasions during the Bush Administration that he requested food to come from my kitchen to his office. The first time the President ordered a red beans and rice dish with fried chicken. He wanted jalapeño cornbread with the meal. We had to make the meal for twelve people he had as guests.

The second time, the President wanted an Italian dish, so we made lasagna with the best beef and pork you could imagine. We made pasta right there in the White House kitchen. We had tomatoes flown in and cooked them down to make the sauce.

We made white and green asparagus and made a Béarnaise sauce to top it. We also made a mixed salad with goat cheese. The President also wanted walnuts and grilled shrimp on the salad. For dessert, we made a chocolate pecan pie with fresh whipped cream on top.

The third and last time the President sent for us to bring food up to the Oval Office, he wanted something much more elegant. We started off with a spinach and strawberry salad. Added to the dish were blackberries, spicy pecans, and goat cheese with a creamy dressing. He didn't want vinaigrette; he wanted a creamy buttermilk dressing.

We made French onion soup and topped it with a sorbet. President Bush started adding a sorbet to his meals because of this first time we served it to him. Traditionally, the sorbet cooks of the White House would keep some of them around. Sorbets were served after the salad and soup to prepare for the entrée.

Next, the President wanted lamb chops flown in from Australia, and we had to make them look like big lollipops. We Frenched the bone with just a little of the round meat at the end of the bone. We roasted red skin potatoes that we cut up in fours, coated them in olive oil, rosemary and thyme, and then roasted them in the oven.

He wanted string beans thrown into the mix because he didn't like peas. He never ate peas while I was cooking for him, and I don't believe he ever ate one pea while I was serving during his one term in office.

This was a meal he had prepared to eat while he was discussing a country he was about to bomb. I was never told which country, but I could guess. It was one of the few times heavy policy discussions were going on that we were not allowed in the room. We did bring the food.

The Secret Service would not let us go in, so we sat the food on tables located outside the doors and stayed there making sure it was all perfectly plated up, and the Secret Service took the food in to serve one person at a time.

I have already mentioned that each President had his favorite snack that he kept on the desk, and President Bush was no different. The strips of beef jerky had to be six inches long and an inch and a half wide. We measured each piece before it ever went up to him. It went into a little glass jar with a lid on it, so that was his snack of the day – every day. We made it fresh every day.

We made the jerky every morning Monday through Friday. On Saturday and Sunday, we didn't put anything on his desk, and we took the jar away. We hand washed it in the kitchen, and then put it in the pantry under lock and key. No one could touch the jar after it was washed except the President's Executive Chef. We made the jerky but were forbidden to put it in the jar.

President Bush's favorite cookie was oatmeal with walnuts and golden raisins. The ingredients were always fresh. The butter came from Paris, the brown sugar from Louisiana, and the flour from the King Arthur Mills located in Vermont. The vanilla we used was imported from Madagascar. The English walnuts came from California where 98% of the world's supply comes from, and they are beautiful nuts. The President did not want the nuts chopped up because he loved the taste of moisture in them. These were no small cookies. They were very large and delicious.

When the children were around the White House, we had to make pizzas. Those people could gobble up some pizzas, and they liked lasagna. We made a lot of lasagna, and I was known as one of the best lasagna chefs in the White House kitchens.

The kids were gourmet French fry eaters. We had a machine in the kitchen that made perfect cuts for fries. We pressed them out and then soaked them in salt for two hours. We placed them in the refrigerator. We pre-fried the potatoes and when the children were ready to come down and eat, we would drop them in the fryers one more time. They were the best fries you could eat. Much better than McDonald's, who used to be known for great fries but not any more.

The President also loved Southern fried chicken, but the food he loved above everything else we made for him was barbecued ribs. Mrs. Bush loved salmon grilled on pecan wood. Everybody needs to try it. Place a piece of pecan wood underneath a slab of salmon. Place dill weed with butter, lemon, and capers on top and put it in the oven. Bake it until it's color turns from pink to a light tan, remove and have one of the most delicious ways to make salmon. Both the Bush's loved snow crab and lobster with clarified butter.

The food I made was the path to the hearts of both President and First Lady Bush. I sensed that maybe I was graduating myself and was now ready for the trip up to Kitchen 2.

CHAPTER THREE
A One on One with the President

I received a personal call from the White House instructing me to be in the Oval Office at a certain time. Whenever the President summoned me, it was always a call to the kitchen. This time it was different. The White House called me at my home late in the evening and ordered me to be in the Oval Office to talk to the President at 10:00 a.m. the next morning.

I couldn't sleep all night. I tossed and turned and finally got up and sat in the living room, so everybody else could get some sleep. My stomach was upset as I was trying to figure out what I did that was wrong. I reasoned that if you get a call like that, you're in trouble and are getting fired.

The only thing I could think of was that I accepted an invitation to talk to some kids at school about what my job was at the White House. I really didn't get permission to do it but didn't think I needed to.

I must have said something wrong during that presentation was the thought pounding in my head. I let those kids know I was an employee at the White House, and what a honor it was to cook for the President of the United States. I told them I was a minority, and it was a wonderful thing to serve the most prestigious and important office in the world, and that our President did not see color when he hired people.

I was so nervous when I walked into the Oval Office, and there stood Ann my sweet wife.

"Annie, what are you doing here?" I said as I walked through the door. I didn't see the President because he wasn't in the room.

"Ronnie," she said, "Don't you know what you did? You don't know?"

"What I did? What did I do?" I pleaded.

"Well I can't tell you. The President is about to come in here, and he will tell you."

"Annie, tell me, please."

"I can't do it Ronnie, and why did you do this?"

I was about to cry or have a heart attack when the Vice President walked through the door. The Chief of Staff walked in followed by First Lady Barbara Bush, and following her was the President of the United States. I stood there shaking and my brow glistened with sweat. I was sick to my stomach.

I got in the habit of taking my hat off when I went in front of the President, so it was sitting in the hallway. I had nothing to hide my nervousness. Sweat ran down my legs and into my shoes. It was that bad. I was standing at attention.

"Ronnie, relax." The President said.

"Mr. President, what did I do? Why am I here?"

"You did something we didn't think you would do." He replied without cracking a smile. "You were out representing our country. You represented our kitchens. You represented your President, your family, and your people. I have something special for you."

"What is that?" I asked as someone completely puzzled as to what was happening.

"You went out saying some things we didn't think you would say. You went out and spoke to some children."

"But Mr. President, I didn't tell no lies. I didn't mess up did I?"

"No, no, no. You did real well, and I have something for you. You're getting a raise, and you're now in Kitchen 2."

I thought this was the end, and what a wonderful shocking surprise to be told you were moving up in front of all these powerful people and my wife.

"How do you like this?" The President asked.

"Mr. President. I'm overwhelmed. I like it a lot. I don't know what to say."

"Chef Seaton, I have something here I want you to have to remember this day."

The President called in a man who was holding a beautiful little box. He opened the box and stood at attention in front of the President. President Bush reached in and pulled out a medal hanging on a red, white, and blue ribbon. As he placed it around my neck, he said:

"I am giving you, Chef Ronnie Seaton, the Freedom Medal. You expressed to those young people what freedom means in this country, and those young people as well as all people will look up to you the rest of your life. I will look up to you."

Through the tears leaking from the eyes of the people in that room, President Bush stuck out his hand, and I shook President Bush's hand for the very first time.

I started crying and he said, "Don't cry."

"But I have to," I exclaimed. "I'm happy."

"Anything you want?" The President asked me.

"Yes," I replied. "I want Ann to come here. Ann, come here, please."

Ann walked up to me smiling through her tears. "You know you got me, you got me good."

Then the First Lady walked up and gave me a kiss on my cheek. The Vice President's wife, Marilyn, also gave me a kiss.

"Mr. President, thank you so much. I will cherish this the rest of my life, but I have to go back to work."

"Ronnie, you take the rest of the day off."

"No sir, I'm going back to work," and so I did.

CHAPTER FOUR
Holidays at the White House
Extra Ordinary Things

Christmas at the White House under every President is special, but Mrs. Bush made it more so than any First Lady I worked with, and she had the full cooperation of her President husband. As I have said, those two worked together in perfect harmony.

I was still in Kitchen 3 and was given the assignment to make edible ornaments. I had not done that before, so I sought the advice of the more experienced chefs and started to work.

They were made from flour and cookie dough, and they were like a decoupage and weren't edible. We stamped those on the back with a warning not to ingest them, but the cookies we made as ornaments were for the pleasure of eating. When the Christmas season was over, we gave them to different orphanages.

The chefs made elaborate gingerbread houses. I didn't get to work on those until later, but I designed and made cookies that were various trees. These cookies were the tress of all 50 states in the US. I also put the state's bird on every tree. These were really elaborate, and I worked long hours on them. When I got to the State bird of Louisiana, the pelican, I made it bigger than any other bird.

I know the pelican is a dufus sort of bird, but he really looked good that day hanging on the Christmas tree. I hung it in the middle where everybody could see it. I was proud of what I'd created.

We also made ornaments that represented the flowers of all

50 states. We had an international tree and a patriotic tree with every ornament the colors of the American flag, red, white, and blue. The chefs loved to decorate those trees; even though, it required extra hours and was so much work.

The gingerbread houses go way back and have been a tradition for a very long time. We had one team of chefs who did nothing else but make those houses, and they had the technique down to a science as the chefs of the past perfected the art.

I loved Easter time as well. The Easter egg hunts on the White House lawn were phenomenal and as I came up the ladder with the Bush White House, I got to display my talents at fancy eggs. I made Faberge eggs out of pastry, and I would place gold leafing on them as the other chefs did making their eggs. We made fresh jellybeans in the shape of eggs. We made Heavenly Hash candy, truffles, and tons of cookies and cakes. One of the most delightful creations the children adored was the life-sized Easter bunny made of cake. That was a masterpiece.

We played games with the kids. We rolled Easter eggs on the lawn and had egg races with a spoon. We played a game without our hats, but in our jackets. We called it "Sack and Chefs."

Mrs. Bush would say, "Let's go!" You thought you were playing in front of your grandmother. When the kids were playing at Easter, she would stop all cooking and pull us out of the kitchen, and we were all out there in our chef jackets and black pants. Everyone was having fun right down to the guys who ran the dishwashers.

The Bush's had family values, so they invited everybody. The Secret Service, stewards, groundskeepers, and all the chefs gathered on the lawn to have fun and play games with their families at the White House. That was one time of the year that we got to see each other. We didn't see each other all the time, and sometimes we would go for a long time without really knowing who was hired on, and who was gone.

Thanksgiving was a wonderful time at the White House, but the public wasn't invited. The meal on Thanksgiving Day was like something from Martha Stewart's kitchen. The golden glazed turkeys, hams, pork tenderloins, potatoes, rice, pasta, and all sorts of vegetables. For dessert, we had all kinds of pies imaginable and a mountain of chocolate that would stand up and run down the mountain, and kids would stick skewers with strawberries into the chocolate.

President Bush was sold out to the country, and that's why he was such a good President. The thing that was the most glaring to the kitchen staff was how close the President's wives were to the decision making of the President. We all knew when the President was stressed or on edge. He looked different, and his mannerisms changed. It was then that you would see Mrs. Bush around him all the time.

The President has said his best advisor was his wife. Mrs. Bush loved children and hated child abuse. She's used to tell us that it is God first, family second, and your job third.

"Take care of your family," Mrs. Bush would say. "Take time to visit your child at school. Take time to have a night out with your wife. Take your family to church."

One time Mrs. Bush found out that my wife was sick. "Ronnie, your wife is sick," she said to me. "Go home and see her and take care of her."

I never heard Hillary Clinton say that to anyone, and I was too new to know if Nancy Reagan ever took an interest in our personal lives, but Laura Bush did, as did Michelle Obama. I am an African American chef, and I loved Mrs. Barbara Bush.

All the Presidents play golf. It's the game of choice, and President Bush was very good at it. He said one time that more deals are made on golf courses than in boardrooms. I don't know if he was talking about United States deals, but I bet he was.

When Presidents go play golf, the chefs go with them because they make the food out there because the Secret Service won't allow them to eat from public places. I did not go out on the course with President Reagan, but I eventually did with President Bush.

We drove a truck out that looked like a U-Haul truck with a kitchen inside, and we made the food in the truck. I was invited to go twice. We weren't cooks on duty; we were the chefs out there. Prior to the event, we met as a committee and discussed what we were going to have on the menu. I had made it by then to the top of Kitchen 3, so when they invited Kitchen 3 to make the food, I got to go help.

The first time I was working the President's golf meeting, he asked for a New York Strip steak with Mediterranean rice and asparagus. We packed tables and silverware, set them up, and served the food.

The second time I was out there, we made hamburgers. We made homemade sesame seed buns. The mayonnaise and ketchup was made from scratch. We sliced all the fresh tomatoes that would be placed on the burgers. President Bush didn't like French fries, so we would fix him hash browns. The dessert was always oatmeal cookies made with golden raisins, walnuts, brown sugar, and Madagascar vanilla. The oats were the old-fashioned kind and not the instant stuff they use today.

The drink of choice was ginger ale. The oldest ginger ale brand in America is Vernors, and sometimes they would drink Schweppes Ginger Ale. President Bush knew the owner of the company, and he donated most of the ginger ale they drank. When a President endorses or uses a product, that's the best advertisement there is.

We also had a side dish as well for those who wouldn't order a steak or hamburger. We made a version of spinach and tomato rusks, and the President liked roasted chicken with avocados, jalapenos, black beans, a little salsa, but no rice. Everybody ate what the President ate, and there was always enough food for seconds if the President had seconds. No one had seconds unless the President did.

The Secret Service was not allowed to eat during the golf outings. We were sensitive to this, so we would pull some food off to the side and put in bags that they would put in their pockets.

The preparation for a president's flight on Air Force One took major planning sessions for the kitchen preparing the food. I didn't get to fly during the Bush administration because I hadn't risen to that level yet. I was involved with some meetings for the flight preparation as far as planning the food and having input from my experiences.

During those meetings, we would brief the staff traveling with the President how he liked certain food prepared that he was going to eat. Also at these meetings were chefs, the Secret Service, FBI, Chief of Staff, and the First Lady. All the First Ladies attended these meetings because they wanted to make sure how things were being handled for the President. They were involved because when the President leaves the White House he may not return, so every trip was high priority.

The President had a private Secret Service made up of four guys. One African American and three Caucasian guys, and those guys don't stop. They can't go home until the President is in his pajamas and in bed. They come back to the White House duty two hours before the President gets up in the morning.

The Secret Service stands guard outside the President's door all night until the relief comes. Then the relief guard comes on. They have a secret knock between them and the President, and he knows it is safe to leave the room and go to work. There is a password as well, so the life of the President in every phase is protected.

President Bush was a real good and honorable President. You had to respect him because there was nothing coming out that would create any other feeling about him. He was consistent, and you never saw him wavering from his firm decisions. He was known as one of the best negotiators of modern times. When he left, we hated to see him go.

I wanted to keep moving up, and I would have made that transition quicker if President Bush stayed on board.

CHAPTER FIVE
First Lady Barbara Bush

The most conservatively dressed First Lady was Barbara Bush. I believe she dressed that way to show her maturity and finesse. She had beautiful white hair that reminded me everyday of my grandmother. Her smile was genuine and infectious. When she would talk to you, she would hold our hand in both of hers. When she spoke to you, you forgot that she was the First Lady, and she made you feel that you were talking with somebody you loved and had known all your life.

Mrs. Bush visited all the kitchens and when she would walk in, the place would glow. She was never too busy to pay attention to what you were doing.

"What are you cooking today?" She would ask. "Can I taste some of that?"

Why would the First Lady ask if she could taste something you were cooking? Of course she could, but she wanted to give you the respect.

"I think you need a little more oregano," she would say.

"Yes, First Lady."

"Oooh, that's right on the mark." This was her favorite thing to say when she liked something you were making.

She would come into my kitchen. "Ronnie, how are we doing?

"I'm doing fine, First Lady. I'm doing better now that you're here." I would tell her.

"So what are we having today?" She asked me.

This meant that she wanted me to taste it with her. "Well

come on, let's see. Would you like to try this?" I asked her when we came to a pot on the stove.

"What is it?"

"Today, we have gumbo," I replied. "New Orleans style."

Mrs. Bush got her sauce and asked, "Where's the shrimp?"

"On the side," I replied.

"Why?"

"I can't put it in there because someone is allergic to shellfish, but if someone wants it, we'll put it in there."

She said, "I want everything you got in there."

I put the shrimp in and then added oysters. We both stood there by the stove eating the gumbo out of a six-inch bowl while the kitchen staff was smiling. The crew gave me a thumb's up. Mrs. Bush polished off her entire bowl and smiled.

The Secret Service walked over and asked if they could have some. When I asked them how much they wanted, they said five gallons. I gave them five one-gallon jars and sent them on their way. The strange thing was I was comfortable enough to do it in front of Mrs. Bush, and she acted like she didn't even see it.

Mrs. Bush was involved with kids. She allowed school kids to come to White House all the time. She read to them. Laura Bush would come also because she was a librarian and would have story time with Mrs. Bush and the children. Mrs. Bush and Laura Bush (who would become a First Lady herself) were reading together – mother and daughter-in-law. It was a beautiful and memorable thing.

Barbara Bush loved spinach and artichoke dip. We made this special for her, and she loved to dip our crackers in the concoction. We made the crackers from scratch. You lay the cracker on a cookie sheet and then sprinkle parmesan cheese on it and then sprinkle cracked peppercorn on it. You place it in the oven and bake. Mrs. Bush used to serve this to lady friends she would have over for tea.

CHAPTER SIX
Memorable Visitors

The person who made us the most nervous that came to the White House was Margaret Thatcher. She came during the Reagan administration, and she was Reagan's best friend, and that transferred over to President Bush. There was no doubt that both Presidents admired her.

It was a very intense atmosphere as every one came together. There were guards all over the place and the Secret Service had an unusual amount of personnel on the premises. This was the American security, and then the guards from England came in.

With all the intensity, the meal went off with no problems whatever. I was in charge of the vegetables because that's what I was known for the most. I made a Bundle of Hope Asparagus. The bundle is tied with a bow made from green onions, and a lemon dill butter sauce poured over the top. The asparagus was white and purple and then tied with the green bow. The main entrée was salmon. On the side was rice with golden raisins and pine nuts. The salad was a Mesclun mix made with heirloom cherry tomatoes. We did a lobster bisque soup and apple pie for dessert. The apple pie was topped with a heavy whipped cream made with confectionary sugar, vanilla, and nutmeg.

The meal was elegant, and so was the table. Rose petals were placed on all the tables. The beautiful candles were lit with wax on the tip. We froze the candles overnight, so they would burn slow. The room was filled with bowls filled with lavender oil and a candle in each bowl. The beautiful display represented the fifty States of the United States of America.

Mrs. Bush looked like an angel. Her white hair so contrasted with her lovely blue dress that it made her look heavenly. President Bush looked like Clark Gable without a mustache. President Bush was dressed in a handsome tuxedo and had the build of an athlete.

Prime Minister Margaret Thatcher was dressed in a gold gown trimmed with a lovely lemma lace embroidery on it. The band played both National Anthems as the important dignitaries came in and sat down.

I was disappointed by not being there for the meal. I was busy in the kitchen making the asparagus bundles, so that the meal could be delivered on time. We always remembered the State dinners, and who came to them, because President Bush only had a handful of them unlike the other Presidents. He did a ton of small dinners while he was negotiating or entertaining in private parties. Kitchen 1 handled all of those dinners.

My greatest disappointment was the two times Margaret Thatcher was visiting the White House under two Presidents, I did not get to meet her. We were able to watch the proceedings on closed circuit TV in the kitchen.

Governor Arnold Schwarzenegger came to the White House. The Governor wanted to visit the kitchens and meet all the chefs. When he came to my kitchen, he surprised me by doing something no one thought he would do. He grabbed me and instead of shaking my hand, he picked me up, and that frightened me. He's a big man.

"Please put me down Governor," I pleaded.

"I just wanted to show you how strong I am," he said.

"I understand how strong you are but please put me down."

He gently and respectfully set my feet on the floor. "Thank you very much," I said. I had remained very calm through the whole ordeal.

Denzel Washington, Sidney Poitier, and Nancy Wilson came to the White House, and I was able to meet them, which was a thrill for me to be in the presence of such big stars. Bill Cosby and Robert Redford also came to visit. Bill Cosby did not hold back cracking jokes and making us laugh. He was fun. Robert Redford wanted to see where the State Department ate, so he showed up at Kitchen 3. He wanted to eat there, so he went through the line like the others. All the girls were giddy at seeing such a handsome and famous man in their kitchen eating the food they helped prepare.

Jerry Lewis came to the White House, and we were enamored by what he was doing for the Muscular Dystrophy Foundation. He was gracious to us when he came to our kitchen.

These are the people I met during the Bush administration. People sometimes ask me, who was my most favorite famous actor/actress that I met. They were all okay but I enjoyed meeting Sidney Poitier the most. The reason? My grandmother's favorite movie was *Lilies of the Field*, and I probably saw the movie a hundred times. I felt like Sydney Poitier was my brother.

Mr. Poitier sang *Amen* right out of the movie. He had everybody singing *Amen*, and it was so special. I get tears in my eyes just remembering how awesome that moment was because it made me remember my grandmother.

George W. Bush, Jr. would come to the White House to visit as would Jeb Bush now and then. The kids came, and they couldn't go to Kitchen 1 or 2 and get anything to eat, so they would come down to Kitchen 3, and we always had pizza, so the sons and families would come over and order pizza.

The grandkids hung around my bakery. I couldn't say no when they asked for something. When we couldn't make something, we would arrange to deliver the goods the next day.

Dan Quayle was a very nice person. He wasn't anything like the media made him out to be; a dufus who couldn't spell. That famous gaff about potato or potatoe? The media made a big deal out of his correcting a child's spelling of the word. We spelled the word both ways in the kitchen.

I didn't see Mr. Quayle very often but when I did, he was always cracking jokes, but he was deadly serious when it came to doing his job, and most people may be surprised about that. He was very athletic and in great shape. He swam a lot, played golf, and liked to run.

The Vice President can't run by himself, so he got about twenty Secret Servicemen in shorts, a tank top, and sneakers, and they would all be out there running. They would get up early in the morning before the public started to work and run on the streets. The Secret Service didn't like it because he was too exposed, and the President tried to get him to run inside, but he wouldn't do it. He said that's what he wanted to do, and he liked running among the people even when some of them didn't like him much.

I talked all the time to the chefs in Kitchen 2 that cooked his food, and they said he didn't have a lot of special requests and was very easy to please. His wife was a vegan, so they dealt with her without too much difficulty. She was the quietest of all the presidential spouses. She stayed totally out of the way, so I didn't know her. At times, the Quayle's would eat in my kitchen depending on what we were serving. If they liked the food, they would come by and tell us.

Vice President Quayle and his wife were very good dancers. Mr. Quayle could really dance and so elegantly, but Mrs. Quayle was not a real fancy dresser. She was plain but very prim. Her name was Marilyn, but the chefs would all say she wasn't Marilyn Monroe. She wasn't a real beautiful lady, but we respected the way she carried herself. She wore two-piece suits and a little pillbox hat that looked out dated, and she was never very much of a public person. That's the way we saw her.

President Bush jumped out of an airplane on his ninetieth birthday. He loved to jump out of planes. That was in 2014, but it didn't go unnoticed in the White House among the staff because he was in a wheel chair and still jumped. They all loved President Bush.

Michelle Obama has contacted all the chefs that worked during the George H. Bush Administration, and they are having a big hoe-down barbecue in Texas in his honor, and I will be attending. I will be making my white chili. I'm famous around the White House for that chili recipe that is still under lock and key. President Bush loved that chili.

CHAPTER SEVEN
President George H. W. Bush's Favorite Meals
How He Liked to Dress

Breakfast

Oatmeal made with brown sugar, heavy cream, cinnamon, and golden raisins, 3 blueberries on top (the blueberries represented the past, present, and future), 2 lumps of sugar

1 banana and the whole banana no longer than six inches

1 small glass of apple juice

1 cup of hot Earl Grey tea with cream and 2 lumps of sugar

Lunch

Turkey on toasted bread with light mayonnaise, swiss cheese, Boston Bibb lettuce, 1 slice of tomato

1 bowl of tomato soup

1 glass of milk

Reagan loved oatmeal cookies – exactly 4 inches in diameter, brown sugar, golden raisins (he didn't like black raisins because he thought they looked like bugs), and walnuts from California.

President Bush only ate exactly 4 ounces of soup, and the turkey was a hot slice of breast freshly cooked.

Fast Foods

The President would send out for Hardy's roast beef with curly fries and au jus with a strawberry milkshake.

President Bush sent out for his fast food, and it was funny because the Secret Service would come back to the kitchen carrying a titanium case with the Presidential Seal.

Favorite Alcoholic Beverage

President Bush only drank red wine for dinner. He was not a social drinker.

How He Dressed

The President wore a blue suit, white shirt, and tie. He liked to dress down a little wearing a sport coat, shirt, and tie. He occasionally wore a golf shirt and slacks, and he was really dressed down when he donned a pair of golf shorts.

★ ★ ★ ★ ★

BUSH, SR.

Menu

•

MEDITERRANEAN SPRING MIX

*with seeded cucumbers, Roma tomatoes, black olives,
and feta cheese with a cold-pressed Italian olive oil dressing*

STEAMED LOBSTER

*with a side of mashed Yukon gold potatoes and
lightly seasoned French string beans.
Golden butter side*

BOSTON CREAM PIE

with vanilla custard, drizzled with chocolate ganache

PREPARATION FOR SIX PEOPLE

SALAD

1 lb. Mediterranean spring mix
2 medium sized cucumbers
6 Roma tomatoes
1.5 cup black olives
1.5 cup feta cheese
1.5 cup Italian salad dressing

DIRECTIONS

1) Skin cucumbers and slice lengthwise down the middle. Remove seeds w/ spoon, cut cucumber in ½" roundels.

2) Stem tomatoes, cut into ¼'s.

3) Mix salad ingredients and serve.

ENTRÉE

4 lb lobster
12 medium sized Yukon gold potatoes
1 stick unsalted butter
1 tsp nutmeg
2 tsp white pepper
1 cup heavy whipping cream
4 egg whites
42 French string beans

DIRECTIONS

1) Place in boiling water for 15 minutes. Remove and pat dry. Place lobster on sheet pan and place in oven at 350 degrees for 20 min. Remove from oven, slice lobster down the middle, remove claws and slice open. Place

tails and claws on plate w/ side of clarified butter*. Melt butter in jar on stovetop, use fat on top.

2) Skin and quarter Yukon gold potatoes, boil in salt water 20 min. Put through ricer.

3) Combine ingredients (1 stick unsalted butter, white pepper, heavy whipping cream). Mix in bowl at medium speed until fully mixed. Place mix in pastry bag w/ star tip.

4) Steam French string beans 17 min. Drizzle w/ clarified butter* and white pepper.

DESSERT

Sponge cake or angel cake mix
Vanilla custard
2 cups heavy whipping cream
8oz grated dark chocolate

DIRECTIONS

1) Top cake w/ custard in cake pan.

2) Melt dark chocolate and mix w/ heavy whipping cream. Pour over cake and custard (should look like glass when hardened.

3) Serve.

SECTION 3
PRESIDENT WILLIAM "BILL" CLINTON

CHAPTER ONE
A Democrat Comes on Board

Everybody was excited when Bill Clinton came on board. We had served twelve years under Republican Presidents, and I was anxious, as we all were, to find out how much difference there would be between the two parties when it came to the operations of the everyday White House living.

President Clinton was a different kind of president, and we all knew it. He was going to be out of the norm. He had a persona and a big smile. He was bringing a new message, and we were excited both Democrats and Republicans in the kitchens. We followed that entire campaign and were doubly shocked when Bill Clinton won the Presidency. None of us expected this to happen.

One of the reasons we were nervous is because we didn't know if we would keep our jobs. If President Bush won the election, there wasn't much worry, but we all knew what could happen when a new regime steps on board. I was one of the many that started updating our resumes.

I was still in Kitchen 3 when the new President arrived at the White House. He came to the White House and visited the kitchens before he took the Oath of Office and was sworn in and brought his wife, Hillary, with him.

The Clintons followed the same protocol as all presidents. When they come to the White House for their visit, they don't stay in the White House. They stay in the Blair Mansion that is the guesthouse of the President of the United States located at 1651 Pennsylvania Avenue NW in Washington, D.C. Many people don't realize this house exists as part of the presidential estate.

The first thing the new First Lady does is walk all through the White House. She starts changing things immediately, and the whole place takes on a metamorphosis. New furniture, drapes, and paint are coming, and the whole place will look different with each presidential family that takes up residence in the White House.

The most important places the presidential couple visits are the kitchens. The President is going to eat from these kitchens, feed his staff, and entertain his dignitary guests. The First Lady will want full control of what comes out of there not only for their dining pleasures, but they want to know who is making these meals. The chefs are revered among the White House families and especially the good ones.

My first encounter as the Executive of Kitchen 3 with the changing of the guard was when we were invited into the auditorium to meet the new President and First Lady along with the Chief of Staffs and the new Vice President. The entire crew from Kitchen 3 was with me. The sous chefs, cooks, stewards, dishwashers, and everybody working in my kitchen were behind me while I was sitting on the front row by myself. That day, we didn't cook at all. We made box lunches, so that we could attend this most prestigious event and have some unforgettable moments to cherish.

We stood at attention as President Clinton walked in and introduced himself. He tells us how happy he is to be there. He cordially says he hopes we all have a lasting and amicable relationship, and that he has an open door policy.

"Anytime you need to see me and want to talk to me for any reason that is important to you, just let the Chief of Staffs know." President Clinton explained. "The Chief will not hesitate to set up a meeting in my office, or I will come to yours."

Once President Clinton had finished his introduction, he stepped down and re-introduced himself to each Head Chef of Kitchens 1, 2, and 3. The President looked at me. (Remember, I am the only African American Head chef.)

"Where you from, Chef?" He asked. "Oh, I know, you're from Nawlens."

"Mr. President, it's New Orleans." I replied.

"Okay," he chuckled, "New Orleans. How's the food down there?"

"Mr. President, it's real good."

"Do you get to cook your type of cookin?" He asked.

"No, Mr. President, I don't make that kind of food here."

"Why's that?"

"Because it's not requested, and I can only cook what's requested."

"Well," groaned the President, "We're about to make some changes."

I am not known as a person who wastes opportunities. I had been struggling with the thought of having to leave the White House after almost twelve years, and my stomach had churned, and I had sleepless nights thinking about the possibility of not having this job anymore.

"Mr. President?" I seized the moment. "May I ask you a question?"

"Sure, shoot," he replied.

"Are you planning on getting rid of me?"

I think everybody in the room gasped at my boldness or maybe my stupidity, but I had to know, and I had to know right then. I could ask for forgiveness later.

"Nope. I'm not," the President said without hesitation. "You're getting a promotion. You are now the Head Chef in Kitchen 2."

He promoted me right on the spot and did it quickly and went on down the line. This whole matter happened inside of a couple of minutes, but I will never forget this, ever.

I mulled over and over the reasons why he would do something like that, and then one of my friends who did get fired told me the truth of the matter. He said that my reputation preceded me, and President Reagan and President Bush had recommended that I be kept on as a chef.

I was a good cook and a good supervisor. My crew almost never missed a day of work and when they did, all the proper documentation was put in well in advance, so that we were never under pressure from someone not showing up for work.

President Clinton told me later that he wanted all the others to see that he did not see skin color, and that he promoted a person based on their character, loyalty, and professionalism. I went from Executive Chef of Kitchen 3 to Executive Chef of Kitchen 2 where I was in charge of the food for the Vice President and all the Cabinet Members that worked for the President.

The entire highlight of that historic meeting for me was when President Clinton pulled one of his stunts that endeared us to him whether we agreed with his politics or not. He put on his sunglasses and nodded to the Secret Service. They brought his saxophone to him, and he played *Happy Days Are Here Again.*

After the President had finished his song, and we all had a great time listening to this different sort of leader, the President said,

"All you single ladies raise your hand."

When nobody did, he asked again, "All you single ladies raise your hands." When they did, he said, "Well, I didn't realize there would be that many single ladies in the kitchens. Good seein ya'all, Bye."

I always wondered how many of those single ladies would become acquaintances with President Clinton down the road. I found out first hand because some of them were in my kitchen. He developed a list and on certain occasions, he would send down a request for a meal and asked that a certain lady bring it up to him.

The meal would be taken to his private dining room in the afternoon during President Clinton's customary break from 3:00 p.m. to 4:00 p.m. Most of the time when the ladies went up, he went back to work around 5:00 p.m. Kitchen 1 would send down a request for a certain ingredient they may be out of and ask for one of the ladies to bring it up. That lady would then take the meal up to the President.

It is very difficult, as I have written already, for a president to conceal anything from his staff. We aren't blind and if the President wants to be naughty, it is impossible to conceal. They know this and because of their power, they ignore all the influences of others and carry on without worrying about it. Sometimes their wives catch them, but that is another story.

CHAPTER TWO
Good Ol' Boy Bill

President Clinton was the most visible of all the Presidents I worked for. You could see him anywhere at any time. He kept the Secret Service in a frantic state most of the time just trying to keep up with him. If he decided in the middle of the night he wanted to take a walk, he would sometimes wind up outside, and many nights his favorite hiding spot was the kitchens.

The President always wanted to know what was being made in the kitchens. It was an every day occurrence for him to keep up with it. He wanted certain things cooked by certain chefs as soon as he learned and zeroed in on the chefs that made the best particular dish he wanted. He didn't always ask his personal chef to make all his meals.

There were a couple of chefs there from Arkansas, so Mr. Clinton would send a message that he wanted a certain food, and he wanted that particular chef to make it. When he wanted a New Orleans dish, he sent the order for me to make it. I was the expert at cooking Cajun style food.

This is how the President and I got close and developed a really good working relationship. As I was with the other Presidents, I never relaxed although it was easier to relax around Bill Clinton than it was President Reagan or President Bush. President Clinton made you feel too much at home, and you would mess up if you weren't careful.

My duties in Kitchen 2 were cooking meals for the Vice President and the Cabinet members. I didn't go to their private residences to cook their meals. We served them breakfast, lunch, and dinner if they were working late, and they ate in the White House. We made meals for the Vice President for his personal residence as well as breakfast and lunch when he was working either at his home or the White House.

I had many duties to perform and was busier than I was in Kitchen 3. When I moved up from Kitchen 3, I brought all my staff with me to our new jobs in Kitchen 2. The former staff in Kitchen 2 scattered. Some of them went down to Kitchen 3, but most of them left their jobs in the White House and ended up in the private sector.

I had twenty-seven employees in Kitchen 3, so I had twenty-seven employees in Kitchen 2. All of them came with me. It wasn't as drastic a change as we first thought it would be. All we needed was to adjust to the new tastes and learn who we would be cooking for on different days of the week.

President Clinton completely changed the way things were done in the kitchens. The whole meal changed to southern cooking, and we abandoned the fancier foods we were accustomed to making. Those French dishes became barbecue everything from beef to pork and chicken.

Southern fried chicken was king. The President loved butter beans, black-eyed peas, and crowder peas. Fried okra was one of his favorites, and he ate a lot of steak. When it came down to it, I don't remember any food Bill Clinton didn't like.

President Clinton loved desserts, and he ate a lot of them. He loved candy, and we had to make the candy from scratch. We made chocolate turtles, but his favorite dessert was chocolate brownies. He couldn't get enough of them. We were making them all the time. Two-inch chocolate brownies with chocolate chunks and pecans in them topped with chocolate icing.

These brownies could not have crumbs falling off them. He kept some all the time in a glass jar on his desk. He sent a warning to anybody that might be tempted to pilfer one of his prized brownies they would promptly be fired on the spot. They were made fresh every morning at 4:00 a.m. and we delivered them to the Oval Office. If he didn't eat one by noon, we picked those up and delivered a fresh new jar.

There were six brownies, all the same size, put in this jar every day because Bill Clinton worked seven days a week. Many times we would deliver food to the Blue Room where he would have meetings way into the night.

Because of my expertise with Louisiana cooking, I would end up working in Kitchen 1 with the Executive Chef there. I would teach him how to make Louisiana cuisine. Out of Kitchen 1, we would make gumbo, etouffee, jambalaya, and boiled seafood.

President Clinton loved fried catfish. I would make it for him with a lump of crabmeat sauce on top. He always said, "It's to die for."

We made German potato salad without mayonnaise, and we seasoned it with vinegar, and he liked it. He would always tell us everyday how much he liked the food, and he was never too busy to stop and talk to you – made you feel special.

President Reagan was never too busy, but George Bush, Sr. was always busy and somewhat unapproachable. Mrs. Bush was never too busy, but Hillary Clinton was impossible to corner for a conversation. You had to get used to all these high-powered personalities if you wanted to survive emotionally. Sometimes, I felt like I was on a pro basketball team.

President Clinton kept his promise to us about being approachable anytime we needed him. If I had a problem with a meal coming up, I would call the Chief of Staff. He would tell me that the President came up for air out of his nap at 3:00 p.m. in the afternoon, and he would see me then.

Bill Clinton took a twenty minute power nap every day. After his nap, he would be as fresh as if he had just slept all night. I would walk into this office, and he would ask me to sit down. He would come over and sit in a chair next to me, and we would have a straight up conversation about what I was doing there.

The President was in no hurry. He would tell me about the kinds of food he liked to eat and ask if I could fix them. He would talk about foreign dignitaries coming to visit, and he would like for the kitchen to be super prepared. He trusted me because I got involved with him early on, and he liked the way I ran my kitchen and my staff. Also, I didn't just supervise. I cooked; even though, I didn't have to, but I liked preparing food for the Presidents and especially one like President Clinton who enjoyed eating.

Apparently, President Clinton was keeping an eye on us and monitoring our moves. The kitchens have microphones in them and security cameras. Microphones were in there in case somebody wanted to talk to you. They are always watching you closely, and the Secret Service never goes away.

I made special things for Mrs. Clinton and their daughter, Chelsea. These were meals that only I would make for them when they wanted them. I actually did the cooking myself, and I believe one reason they liked me was because as a supervisor, I didn't push the food off to someone else. I actually did the work by myself. Of course, they could watch me doing it if they wanted, and I think at times they did.

CHAPTER THREE
Laid Back Bill

President Bill Clinton had some out of the ordinary habits the other Presidents did not have. He would have late night meals, and he had them all the time. He would order food at midnight and later. If he told you he was having special guests, you had to hang around and cook.

President Clinton would bring in lady friends, businessmen that talked over deals, and investors looking towards his next campaigns. We were never in the presence of these people, but we knew who they were by the names on the guest lists.

I was fascinated by how many large corporations that came over to hang out with the President. It was like the scenes from Forbes or Fortune magazines. We would sometimes be around until 1:00 a.m., and my staff would stay with me off the clock to make sure everything was ready for the next day's work.

President Clinton was extremely friendly and went out of his way to make you feel that he really liked you. He treated everybody the same. You would see him walk out of his office with his glasses down on the bridge of his nose, his jacket left in the office, his shirt sleeves rolled up, necktie loose around his neck, and he always had a pad and pen ready to take notes.

One of the major differences between Bill Clinton and the other Presidents was the way his staff dressed for work. Nobody in President Reagan's or President Bush Senior's office was dressed any less than in professional business attire. They dressed that way and demanded the respect of the office they occupied. President Jimmy Carter was the first to wear a sweater with a tie, and that was a major departure from the norm the public was used to seeing.

President Clinton had staff people that dressed in blue jeans, shorts, and tennis shoes. Some of the public touring the White House didn't like this because of the traditions they were accustomed to expecting out of the White House staff. President Clinton brought a slew of young people. There were more youth on the staff than ever in the history of the White House.

President Clinton did have some rules. He wanted the staff dressed properly when the public was around, but they could dress about anyway they wanted otherwise. That rule was not always enforced. Also, if they were on the White House lawn, they had to be dressed in the proper attire.

Bill Clinton was laid back, so everybody liked him. He would be dressed in total casual clothes on the weekends. Whatever he felt like wearing, he wore it. He sported sunglasses, tank tops, tee shirts, shorts, blue jeans, tennis shoes, or sandals. He was a real cool President.

President Clinton was laid back all right, but he also had another side to him that showed up now and then. He had no toleration for incompetence. It wasn't often that you would see him off the track of being in a good mood, but one day I was walking down the hallway carrying some food. Mr. Clinton came out of his office. He has a fairly large nose, and it turns blood red when he's angry. This was the first time I'd seen him this way although I'd heard about it.

He was looking for the person who was late getting important documents for him to sign.

"You stupid idiot!" The President screamed loudly. He was not using profanity. "I'm the leader of the greatest free country on earth, and you mean you didn't bring these documents to me because you went to lunch? What are you thinking? You're fired!"

The Secret Service came quickly and escorted the lady out of the building. I knew her. She worked for the Vice President as an undersecretary, and they got her out of there quickly. We found out the document was going to Russia, and that was why he was anxious.

I never saw him upset like that again until the Monica Lewinsky affair was found out. Other than this one time, I always saw him happy and cracking jokes. He had this little crack of a smile, and he would come up to you and say, "Good job, good job."

He once said that he was the first black President because he grew up around poor African American folks in Arkansas. He detested their poverty and their upbringing. He wanted to do something about all that, so he became the Governor of Arkansas. We had people in the kitchen who came from Arkansas, and they would talk about what a great Governor he was.

President Clinton had the persona about him that attracted the ladies to him. Maybe he wasn't exceptionally handsome, but he had that personality. He was friendly. There was no one he wouldn't talk to, and nothing he wouldn't talk about. He was intelligent, so no one really challenged him; they listened to what he had to say.

We were always carrying food through the hallways where the President would be coming in and out or moving here and there. We would see him stop and talk to anyone that spoke to him. All you had to say was, "Good morning, Mr. President," and he would stop and talk to you and ask how your day was going.

I learned that the President wouldn't raise his hand to stop the Secret Service following him down the hallways. When he wanted to talk to somebody, he pinched his left ear. That meant he wanted the Secret Service to stand still until he finished talking to whomever it was he wanted to engage in a conversation. I can tell you that neither of the previous two presidents I worked for had these habits. It wasn't because they weren't amicable and nice men; they weren't socializing with the working crowd moving throughout the White House.

CHAPTER FOUR
Beyond Protocol and Monica Lewinsky

I was the Executive Chef over Kitchen 2, so I worked directly for Vice President Al Gore. The only time I cooked meals for President and Mrs. Clinton was when they requested something they wanted me to cook.

Elvis Presley's favorite desert was a fried banana, so President Clinton would ask that I make it for him because Elvis had shared it with President Richard Nixon. He liked peanut butter with it, and he ate a lot of them. He also liked the soups that I made. There is an art to making good tasty soup, and not every chef can do it.

The President was a lover of real Mexican burritos. I could make burritos and rice pilaf, and the Clintons would have me make those for them now and then. Veggies are also my specialty so even though I didn't cook the meat or main entrée such as seafood, he would request my veggies on the side. These encounters with the President, Mrs. Clinton, and their daughter gradually helped build a trust, respect, and great relationship with them.

As a Head Chef in the kitchens, you were constantly being subjected to things you really didn't want to know about much less witness. President Clinton's own charismatic personality was also his worst enemy. I am not a reporter or a biographer, but I observed things that bothered me about my President. One of the main things was his affinity for the opposite sex. I don't have to document any of this because it's common knowledge.

What isn't common is the perspective that comes from those people who were around the aberrations of the Presidents every day. Those observations are more than gossip; they're a reality, and it is sometimes difficult to understand how a man who is the President of the greatest country in the world, and holds the number one position on the planet was so comfortable allowing casual acquaintances to become a social nightmare for everybody involved or not involved. I can only speak of those things I observed myself and since I am telling my story, I will tell everything that affected me except for classified information.

President Clinton received some guests. One was a lady who was a publisher, but I don't remember what company she represented. She had come to the White House and stayed a couple of nights. President Clinton entertained her in his private dining room for dinner.

Bill Gates and his wife came to visit the next evening for dinner. They weren't in there long before Mrs. Gates went storming out because the President told a joke she didn't appreciate. Bill Gates stayed a couple more hours after his wife left.

President Clinton was entertaining a President from a country in South America. We saw the President leaving in a hurry not long after they arrived, and we were told that the President gave the man's wife a pat on the butt. We were told that the South American dignitary raised his hand like he was going to smack President Clinton in the side of the head. The Interpreter calmed him down and got the gentleman and his wife out of there before anything serious got going.

President Clinton wasn't the most discreet person in the world. Many times we would bring food to the Clintons and half of the Clinton family wasn't there. Instead, there would be an unrecognizable lady sitting at the table across from him. Mrs. Clinton did a lot traveling, so it opened up the opportunity for the President to party a little.

Mrs. Clinton had a lot of initiatives she was working on. She was embroiled in trying to get her health care planned passed.

She also started "No Child Left Behind," but it didn't go any-where until President George Bush, Jr. got it passed when he was in office.

Through the years, a lot of people have asked me how he got away with some of the stuff he pulled, and the First Lady didn't find out about it. He seemingly was unafraid that every-body would find out about it and tell on him.

Of course everybody knew about it because it happened un-derneath the noses of the Secret Service and the kitchen serving the food. The Secret Service swears allegiance to the President, so there's no danger there for any trouble. The kitchen staff wanted to keep their jobs, so everybody kept quiet for the most part and certainly stayed away from Mrs. Clinton.

Was President Clinton embarrassed at all by his behavior? He was not because he told everybody right from the start that he liked women. It was a weakness so deal with it. From what we all understood, he had all the same problems in Arkansas. Mrs. Clinton found out about his affairs when he was Governor, and those brought some big time troubles for him.

The President couldn't live forever without his wife find-ing out about some of it, and she did, but she kept it from him that she knew about his playing around and cheating. We didn't hear about his right away, but then the gossip started spreading all over the White House that Mrs. Clinton had caught her hus-band cheating on her. They tried to keep as much of it from their daughter as they could, but Mrs. Clinton wasn't one to hold her tongue very long.

We would see the President leaving at odd times with the Secret Service. He would come back smiling, but Mrs. Clinton would still be upset. The next morning we would bring the Pres-ident's breakfast to him in another part of the house.

The most famous affair of any President including John F. Kennedy's well-known escapade with Marilyn Monroe was the Monica Lewinsky matter. She came to the White House, but we didn't know she was the lady that was dining with him some.

We were all curious about her, and we were told that she

was an intern and was working on a project for the university she was attending. We were curious as to why she disappeared and never seem to come and go by the common entrances and exits. I pushed this off as my imagination. Coming through the tunnel that the public was not aware of was not that uncommon, but it would be for this girl unless she was somebody highly classified that they wanted out of the public eye. At any rate, we passed it off as not being that big of deal until later when all hell broke loose.

A special request came down that there was to be a dinner for two in the President's dining room. Of course, we thought it was for the President and the First Lady. We knew it wasn't their anniversary, so we immediately thought it was a "make-up" dinner.

When we looked at the book, Mrs. Clinton's name wasn't on the roster and in fact, she was out of town. At the top of the list was "Mr. President and his Guest." Her name was not exposed, but the fact she was female was disclosed.

I think one of the most seductive meals I've ever helped make was the one we made for the President and his "guest" that night. We served our famous spinach salad with strawberries. Chocolate covered strawberries were put on the side. Lobster bisque soup was served along with a tangerine sorbet. The entrée was lamb chops with the Jacqueline Kennedy duchess potatoes and foie gras as an added feature. Long stem white asparagus was the vegetable, and a chocolate pecan pie for dessert. Caviar was served with toast points. They had a very expensive bottle of Champagne to toast and drink.

I thought, *Wow! This is an expensive meal!*

I got selected to make the food along with a chef from Kitchen 1. We were warned that in no uncertain terms were we to reveal anything about what was going on that night. We were going to cook the meal in a private kitchen. Just outside the President's residence, there is a little kitchen. The chef and I were to be finished cooking at 6:00 p.m., and we were to let the Secret Service know when it was prepared and ready to serve.

This particular dinner was absolutely beautiful, and we had created a masterpiece that would make a king blush. We let the Secret Service know we were ready, so we started to bring the meal to the dining room. The Secret Service stopped us at the door and wouldn't let us go in.

"But we normally bring the food in and set it up the way the President likes it." I said.

"We'll take care of it," the Secret Service guy said.

When we hesitated as if confused, another guy standing and watching said, "What part of NO don't you chefs understand? You have to leave here so go."

We left. We went home fully aware that we would have to be back to work at 3:00 a.m. because all the supervisors have to do a walk through and check the production sheets, make last minute changes if any, and get prepared for the crew that arrives at 5:00 a.m.

We immediately thought of the dining room. We would need to get back up there to make sure everything was emptied out, and all the dishes plus the flatware was back where it belonged. When we arrived, the dishes were sitting on a cart outside the room, but everything wasn't there that was supposed to be.

I opened the door to the dining room and walked in. *What a mess,* I thought. It looked like a wild party went on in there. One of the Secret Service men walked out with a dress on a hanger wrapped in a cleaners bag. It was a dark blue garment.

"Ooh that dress," I commented. "It's really long."

"Yeah, we have to take it to the cleaners," the man answered. "It's got a stain on the chest."

"A stain?" I didn't think much about it.

We were cleaning up when one of the Secret Service guys, who was my friend, came through. He was from Louisiana and graduated from Grambling University.

"John," I said, "What happened here?"

"The President had a little party last night, Ronnie."

"A party?" I asked incredulously. "It was only two people."

"A lady came over last night, and she stayed a long time," he explained. "The President told us to leave the room, go down the hall, and don't even stand by the door. There was a party for sure. She had to leave in a sweatshirt and sweatpants, and we have to take this dress and clean it."

"Don't tell me any more, please." I begged. " I don't want to know anymore about this."

The plates were on the table, but the pillows were everywhere that sat on the sofas and chairs. The fluted glasses of Dom Perignon Champagne containing strawberries were knocked over, and the bubbly had run all over the tablecloth. The bottle had completely emptied itself. Lamb chop bones were all over the floor, and I had never seen anything ever messed up this much in the White House during my time there.

They came in with a steam cleaning crew to try and mop up the mess. Mrs. Clinton was coming back in two days, so they completely changed everything. I went back in the room later, and you couldn't tell anything ever happened. They changed the furniture saying a stain was on the love seat that wouldn't come out.

Not long after, Monica came up the President's office with a group of college students to speak to the President. She was smiling from ear to ear.

The President walked over to Monica, singled her out, and kissed her on the cheek. We were thinking, *of all the women who showed up, he picks this one out and kisses her on the cheek. Hmmm.* We were wondering what in the world was going on because the President never kisses anyone on the cheek.

Mrs. Clinton walked in and stood near the group. Her eyes were piercing. Monica said she needed to use the bathroom and left the room. We heard her tell the President because we were standing right by them. None of us in the kitchen knew much about the affair although we would see her around the President quite often. She came to the White House under cover by using the underground entrance that was a tunnel leading into the main house.

Food was being brought up on trays by the kitchen crew, but

they weren't allowed to go into the Blue Room because only the Head Chefs were allowed in there. Myself and two other chefs were walking into the room at the precise moment that Mrs. Clinton said, "Bill, I need to talk to you."

Everything went on hold, and the Secret Service told us to put everything down and wait outside. We then heard screaming and yelling through the door. Mrs. Clinton was throwing "F" bombs at the President like a rocket launcher. She called him a no good "mother f-----g SOB" and screamed that he had let his whore come into the White House.

After Mrs. Clinton had thrown the major portion of her fit, she opened the door and smiled at us.

"Please come in," she said.

We got out of there. We dropped everything and got away from her. We didn't stop until we had gotten all the down to the kitchen.

It wasn't long until the gossip that was going around the House about Bill Clinton and this intern having a hot affair started becoming a reality. We began to hear about the President heading for impeachment hearings. It was serious business that got our attention and kept our antennas up.

Hillary Clinton found out about Monica Lewinsky, and it hit the fan. We were bringing breakfast in the morning she lit him up one side and down the other. She was screaming at him and telling him that she wanted to be President someday, and he had ruined her life and every chance she was ever going to have. She told him he was not going to lose the Presidency over some bimbo intern because he couldn't keep his member in his pants.

Mrs. Clinton would not hold her tongue when she was angry with anyone. She would flair up and launch into a fit of rage. She didn't care who was around. We heard a lot from the Clinton's, but we kept our mouths shut.

I heard her chew out a chef one time because he dropped a fork. She lit him up because he didn't have another fork ready. He shouldn't have dropped the fork because she was ready to eat. She made him walk twenty feet to get another one. It only took about ten seconds, but it didn't matter, and she yelled at him. Later, he was out of the kitchen and working somewhere else.

President Clinton's trial affected all of us because we didn't know if we would keep our jobs. In that position, you are on edge a lot of the time because things change really quickly. If Al Gore took over, there would be no problem with me staying because he had already said if he got elected President, my job would not be in jeopardy.

CHAPTER FIVE
Hillary Clinton

When Bill Clinton came on board, there were many changes and mainly because of his wife. The First Ladies have a lot of influence about what happens in the day-to-day operations of the White House. I met her when she came down to Kitchen 2. She seemed like a really charming lady and had a nice smile. Her daughter, Chelsea, was with her. Chelsea was quiet and reserved, well mannered, intelligent, and we all liked her.

The Clintons got settled in, and everything concerning the establishment was going really well until one night lightning struck from out of nowhere as the First Lady went off like a nuclear bomb.

I was in Kitchen 2 preparing lunch for the Vice President and Cabinet members. A call came down from Kitchen 1 that prepares the food for the President and family. Mrs. Clinton wanted lobster, and the Executive Chef didn't have it, so he had sent up word that she needed to order something else. That didn't go well, and the First Lady told the chef that he better come up with some lobster, or it would be hell to pay. It didn't take long after the Clintons moved in for us to find out what we were going to be dealing with.

The chef in Kitchen 1 called me to ask if I had lobster, and then told me the predicament he was in. He said he was going to be fired and needed help. He also had been told that I had lobster. I did have lobster, so I told him to send somebody for it, and I would help him out. It wasn't easy to change a menu, but I was able to do it, and nobody was the wiser.

Mrs. Clinton wanted to know where the lobster came from, so my name got attached as being the one who saved the day. Mrs. Clinton came down to my kitchen to meet me.

"Tell me something about yourself," she said. "Are you married? Do you have children?"

I told her about me and where I came from, and that I really appreciated the job and was loving every minute of it. "I'm from New Orleans," I explained.

"How well do you cook?" She asked.

"Well, First Lady, I won't lie. I'm still learning."

"No, no." she commented. "You wouldn't be this high on the food chain if you weren't a good cook."

"Everyday is a new day," I replied. "I have some food now if you would like to taste some."

She said she would, so I gave her some of my lasagna. This was serious lasagna, too. It was made with pork and beef. She wanted to know where the pasta came from, so I told her everything she eats is made from scratch.

"Nothing in my kitchen comes out of a can or a box," I told her. "Everything you eat is made from scratch on the day we serve it"

Mrs. Clinton tasted my food. "This is fabulous," she said. "Can you make this for me?"

"Do you want it now, a hour from now, when?" I beamed.

"Friday," she said.

This was on Tuesday, so I had plenty of time. "How many people?"

"About twenty. Do you think you could make Brussels sprouts to go with it?"

I did the meal, and it blew her away. I made the Brussels sprouts with bacon, cracked pepper, and Kosher salt cooked in olive oil. This started a relationship between the two of us, and I got to see Mrs. Clinton up close and personal.

The main thing about her was she could be mean. She had no problem jumping on anybody she felt was in her way. She would tell all of us exactly how she felt about what we cooked, and that was mainly what she didn't like and rarely about what she did like.

The Congressmen hated to visit when she was around because she would let them know what her title was. She let them know who her husband was, and she kept a book on every one of them. I'm talking about the dirt in their lives. She knew who was taking kickbacks, who was cheating on their wives, and any other sordid thing she could find out and keep records concerning.

Mrs. Clinton was difficult to work for. She was a demanding taskmaster. The impression that the others and I had of her in the beginning proved to be a ruse. I could handle it because of the military training, but some of the others had a difficult time with her.

I had inside connections so when the First Lady was headed down to see me, I already had the answer because my connection would tip me off as to what she wanted. I beat her at her own game. She fired many, many people working in the White House, and I was determined not to be a casualty.

I always felt sorry for the speechwriters Mrs. Clinton employed. She would light them up many times before a speech and would make them change things at the last minute because "that's not what I wanted to say."

She would light up her husband. She would jump him in a heartbeat without worrying about any sort of retaliation from him. He was afraid of her because she had too much on him from years of marriage.

Two chefs, a Sous Chef, and I got a call to cook and bring food to the Clinton's private residence. The President and Mrs. Clinton were alone because Chelsea was at school. We just arrived and were barely inside the door when Mrs. Clinton did a roundhouse wind up and slapped the President across the face and at the same time, called him a liar.

We looked at each other, and said what we were thinking. "We better get out of here!"

The Secret Service said, "No, no, bring that food in here."

We placed the food on the table, and then they told us to stand aside. We were in the line of fire and knew that the President must have done something really off the wall to bring out this kind of wrath from the First Lady.

"But Hillary, I didn't mean to say that, I'm sorry." The President opined.

"You're a damn liar dammit," she fired back and then ran up the stairs.

"Come on fellas," Mr. Clinton said to us. "Serve the food. It's fine. I've been hit before, and I'll keep on being the President."

We set the food out and headed back to the kitchen. We were warned that we better never say a word about this as long as we worked in the White House. I worked many more years and never told this story until this chapter of my life is being told.

Two days later, Mrs. Clinton called the four of us to her office. She explained that she is a woman, and there are times when women get upset about something that normally may not bother them that much. She pleaded with us to keep what we witnessed quiet, and then she apologized.

Mrs. Clinton said she was so sorry that happened in front of us, but she's married to the man. We said in unison, "Yes ma'am."

We were walking towards the kitchen, and the Sous Chef commented, "She never apologized for slapping him."

Mrs. Clinton put on two faces all the time. You had to be with her on both fronts in order to know her. When she was in public, she put on that presidential smile to her husband and acted like she adored him, but when she came into the building, and it didn't matter where in the building she was, she would jump all over the President and embarrass him. He never said a word in his own defense when this was happening.

One time after we brought food up to the residence, Mrs. Clinton hurled a vase at the President. It barely missed him, and if he hadn't ducked, it could have been very serious.

I heard rumors that when Mrs. Clinton didn't like a certain food that was prepared, she would throw the food all over the place destroying the meal. I only witnessed this behavior twice.

Those times, she freaked out and flipped over trays of food. My crew and I had to clean up the messes.

I heard the First Lady say to the President, "I wear the pants around here not you."

I said that the President didn't react to her outbursts, but I meant that he didn't react by retaliation or confrontation. We saw him cry. He did cry when he was hurt like that and embarrassed by the tirades of the First Lady. We often wondered why he didn't control her, but I suppose he couldn't, or he would have. Rumors were she controlled him through information she could hold against him, and he couldn't afford the risks. It's a good question that perhaps history will someday answer.

When the President was Governor, the State Troopers protected him and when he got to the White House, he enlisted the Secret Service to play the same role, and they did. Hillary Clinton knew all about this, but her dream was the White House. She has an insatiable desire to be President of the United States. I believe by her actions that Mr. Clinton's terms were just a steppingstone in the process of Hillary's quest for the White House.

Mrs. Clinton was casual. She didn't demand business dress in the White House. Many times, I thought that short shorts and spaghetti straps were disrespectful to the office, but she didn't seem to care, and the President certainly didn't.

As time moved on into the second term, Mrs. Clinton became very disrespectful to the staff. We called her the "White House Bitch." She would go off for no apparent reason and bang her fist on a desk.

President Clinton prayed in public, but his wife never did. He would pray with his staff before a big meeting, a press conference, and before he met with an important dignitary. He said that's the way he was raised by his mother.

Mrs. Hillary never bowed her head during these prayers or closed her eyes when she was present. You would mostly see her looking around and maybe at her watch. She seemed bored with it all and completely cold toward Spiritual things. I didn't think she had much of a religious upbringing, The President and the

First Lady were members of different denominations, with the President a Southern Baptist, and Mrs. Clinton a Methodist.

I never thought she would make a good President, but that was her aspirations, and I think she would do almost anything to anybody to get there. She had some serious issues, and the reason President Obama didn't choose her as his Vice President is because of her husband's past record. Mrs. Robinson, Michelle Obama's mother, didn't want Hillary Clinton as Vice President with Mr. Obama.

As part of the historical record, I would never vote for Mrs. Clinton for any public office because I've seen her erratic and unexplainable behavior. I will not deny that some of it was because of her husband, who arguably was the biggest wife cheating President in United States history. You learn a lot working around the White House, and I survived because I suppressed any thought of ever giving my opinion about anything while I was on the Government payroll. I did my job and waited until the opportunity would come, and it did. I am an African American, Catholic, and a Democrat, but I wouldn't vote for her.

I know that I will be criticized, and people won't believe me, but I saw Mrs. Clinton throw things. I saw the pieces of the broken vase she hurled at the President and heard the first hand stories of others who witnessed her behavior.

I saw her flip a tray and cuss out her husband. I witnessed her screaming at the top of her lungs at her husband and her daughter. Staff members were afraid of her because no one knew what she would do. You shouldn't shake when your superior walks into the room. Mrs. Clinton forgot who she works for. Her husband works for the taxpayers. The Presidents are not kings, and Hillary Clinton was not a queen.

I am a Catholic, so I don't agree with her views on pro-life. My wife almost died having our last baby, and I'm not sure whether Mrs. Clinton would abort a baby or not, but she pushes the wrong ideas about abortion in my opinion and influences a lot of people to murder children.

I don't respect her views on alternative lifestyles. I do not support Gay Rights or anything about forcing laws on the public that make you accept something I believe is fundamentally against human nature and the Laws of the Bible.

This is an unusual book. There are many books written by people who worked in the White House, but no one worked as long as I did. Everybody looking at this book – the promoters, the publicists, and the public must understand that there are years of pent up emotions. I loved my job, and I am grateful for the opportunities to have served in the White House for the greatest country in the world, and the greatest office in the world.

CHAPTER SIX
State Dinners

The State dinners are prepared out of Kitchen #2, which is the largest kitchen in the White House. The first thing in the preparation is for the chef in charge of the dinner to have a game plan. The whole affair from beginning to end is distributed to the entire staff that will be involved.

These dinners are large and have to be super organized. I was involved with many of them. The second thing is to get your crew together. You have a meeting and discuss the meal, and who is going to be cooking certain things. Those chosen are the best in preparing that certain food. Chefs are chosen to prep the meal, others for doing the actual cooking, the chefs that will handle each course, and then the food is ordered that will come into the White House.

When the groceries were delivered, they were checked out by running through an X-Ray machine and other checks and balances were initiated by the Secret Service to make sure someone was not trying to poison the President. The food is scrutinized at the highest standards to keep the President safe.

The food is then put into walk-in coolers and placed on speed racks. Some of the food is blanched, and then it comes time for the meal. We did not get to go home for a week when one of these dinners was being served at the White House. We stayed in dormitory styled facilities until the whole affair was done.

A waiter out of the kitchen had to be in great shape, and all of them were. They would practice using trays with ten bricks on the tray to represent the weight of the ten plates they would carry to the diners. A guy ahead of them would be carrying a table jack. All the food was served at one time because the waiters carrying the trays set them down in perfect synchronization. I don't know anywhere in the United States where this large of a group is served quite this way. Waiters come in unison with a tray and serve it. They go back and fill their trays with a different course and serve that.

The waiters walk on their heels and not on their toes. Walking on your toes while carry trays of food will make you bounce. All the waiters at the White House are the same height. Not one is taller or shorter than the other. The crew wears the same colors; black and white. The chef's jackets are white, and the pants are black. Only the supervisors are slightly different. Their jackets have a black trim.

The kitchen staff has certain standards that are strictly adhered to. You cannot have earrings in your ears. You are not allowed to wear a watch or a ring. Every two hours, you wash your hands with soap, dry your hands with a paper towel, and put sanitizer on them.

The kitchens have large staffs in order to make something like this happen. We bring in special people who are experts at training the whole staff to put on this kind of affair. After the dinner, the stewards that have been waiting in one of the side rooms come in and knock it all down, clean it up, and have the entire dining hall ready for the next big dinner just like nothing ever happened. It is an amazing feat, and they do it all in two hours.

The Executive Chef of Kitchen #1 is responsible for the entire event. He makes one plate, a photograph is taken, and all the plates must look exactly as he made it from the first waiter to the last.

Making an undertaking of this magnitude happen requires precision timing. The food is placed on the plates before it ever leaves the kitchen. Plates are run down a conveyor belt, and the different food is placed on the plates in the exact order to be carried up to the dining hall. There are people on both sides of the conveyor working. Each person has a certain task even to the placing on of sauce if the meal calls for it.

At the end of the line are expediters. The job of these people is to wipe the plate if anything has spilled, put the plate under a dome, and then place it in a hot box. The hot box is 275 degrees, so the food is not cooked all the way. If we did cook it all the way with the sternos in there, the sauce would break, the food would deflate, and the meat would over cook. It may sound strange, but by the time the food gets to the table, the plate is warm, the food is warm, and the meal is perfect.

We worked for weeks timing the meal to perfection. We had choreographed our presentation down to ten seconds. The President representing the United States of America would put his best foot forward for the Heads of State from these foreign allies. All the Presidents concurred that these super dinners with some of the best chefs assembled in the world could change the course of history. This is why so much expense and detail is spent because good food makes people happy.

We cooked ten percent more food than we needed because something might break, drop, or fall to the floor, and you have something to substitute. The food that was left over from those big State dinners, and the excess food that was prepared for the kitchen staff that was sequestered in the White House during the week that the dinners were being prepared was boxed up and taken to the homeless shelters around the city.

CHAPTER SEVEN
Party President

President Clinton loved the game of basketball and loved to play basketball. He played on a church team when he was growing up in Hot Springs, Arkansas. He invited a group of NBA All Stars to come and visit the White House. These guys drove up in some of the most exotic cars I've ever seen, and there were ladies being escorted with them.

This was going to be a party like nothing I've seen while working in White House kitchens. We set up carving stations with steamship rounds, turkeys, roast beef, hams, and even caviar. We made toast points with the caviar, and nine to the pound shrimp. We made pates and all kinds of dips. This was the most eloquent and extravagant buffet's I ever had a part of creating.

The President surprised us when he walked onto the dance floor. He "cut a rug" as the expression goes meaning he could really dance. In fact none of the kitchen staff had any idea Mr. Clinton could dance like he did that night.

Mrs. Clinton wasn't at this event, so the President's first dance was with a beautiful African American lady. He grabbed her, dipped her, spun her around, and was showing his skills in every way he could. He danced all night with every woman there who wanted to dance with him. That was pretty much all of them because who didn't want their chance to dance with the President of the United States.

The party started at 6:00 p.m. and stopped rolling at 4:00 a.m. the next morning. Most of the NBA players were so intoxicated that they had to leave their exotic automobiles parked at the White House and caught a cab to take them to their hotels. The champagne flowed and flowed. There were ten different bars and bartenders serving rounds and rounds of drink that was on the house – The White House.

A basketball goal was brought in, so that the players could have a slam dunk contest. All the players were dressed up to the nines, and then they removed their shoes and changed to basketball shoes they brought with them. The slam dunk contest began, and the President attempted and made a three point shot to the delight of everyone. The ladies became the cheerleaders, and this party was on.

There is a gymnasium in the White House, and this is where the party was happening. Lots of people ask me all the time about who pays for all these activities. They are horrendously expensive, but not a thought is given for the cost. The President has an unlimited expense account, and the Clinton's were known to use and abuse it. All paid for by the taxpayers of the United States. The President pays for nothing, and he has an unlimited expense account for many things, and one of the biggest is for food and entertainment. I could say food and entertainment budget except there is no budget. A budget is a plan for spending money but in the case of the President of the United States, there is no accounting or budget on these kinds of expenses.

It's expensive. If there is a bomb scare, the Secret Service closes the kitchen, and all the food is left cooking on the stoves. Many times we've come back to burned up food and ruined pots. We break out new cookware and throw the old stuff away.

The First Ladies all have their own crystal and china. They hand select every piece. The dishes are washed in the kitchen on a conveyer that pulls the dishes through and cleans them. The dishes are then sanitized and dried by air. No hands touch the clean dishes. They are put in plastic containers, wrapped with plastic wrap, and then sealed in a air tight container. No one can get to these dishes randomly because the Secret Service locks them up.

This is a good time to explain what safeguards there are to protect not only the President but everyone working in the White House. Protein is not frozen, and the vegetables are now grown in the White House nurseries. Prior to the indoor gardens, each individual piece of food whether it was a single green bean or a melon were x-rayed and then put into containers and brought into the kitchens.

There was an incident while I was working for President Clinton. Someone tried to poison him by injecting acid into a watermelon with a needle. It was found when the Secret Service noticed the melon was starting to shrink while sitting on the dock. They thumped it, and when the sound was not quite right for a ripe watermelon, they cut a piece of it and ran some tests. They found that it had a corrosive acid substance in it. Consequently, all the watermelons went through the same tests. Nothing was found, but they threw them all away and brought in a new shipment. The truck bringing the melons did not stop at the gate but came all the way into the facility.

Poisoned raw chicken was another ploy to harm the President. The chicken somehow made it into the kitchen, and it was then we noticed the chicken changing color. We immediately pulled the chicken and sent it over to the Secret Service. I never heard the results of the test except the chicken was full of poison. God must have been watching over President Clinton because all those close calls were foiled because something out of the ordinary caught our attention every time.

You can see why the chefs are background checked, and checkups occur all the time throughout their careers. Their character must be impeccable. There is a system there called "Has Set." It's essentially a system of handling the food. To get a Has Set designation, you must take a two hundred question test about how to store all sorts of food, how to cook it, and how to preserve it.

I have the International Has Set designation, which is knowledge about how food is cooked around the world. When I was working on my Ph.D., I was experimenting with how to cook food under all kinds of conditions. Being prepared is the utmost responsibility of a chef cooking for the President of the United States.

One of my most favorite memories about President Clinton happened on a day when every person working in Kitchen 2 was super busy. I was working on a picnic, so we were getting everything ready. Fried chicken, barbecued ribs, baked beans, corn on the cob were the stables for a Bill Clinton picnic.

The Secret Service is dressed in Hawaii shirts with long pants. Of course they all have their sunglasses on. To our surprise, President Clinton walks in the kitchen dressed for the picnic. He has on sandals, shorts, tank top, sunglasses, and he's carrying his saxophone. He sounded like Kenny G. or Boots Randolph.

He said to me, "Chef Ronnie, you got my favorite fried chicken?"

"Yes, Mr. President," I replied happily.

"I got a new song for you."

"Mr. President, you got everybody stopped working in here. Don't you have a country to run?" I teased him a little.

"Chef," the President replied, "I know you're from New Orleans and appreciate a good jazz song. I thought I'd just come down and have a little fun. Who are the new interns in here?"

"Mr. President, don't ask me that."

"It's okay, Ronnie, Mrs. Clinton is upstairs. Now who are the new interns? I want them to bring my food outside?"

"Mr. President, you're going to get me in big trouble."

The President played another song and then left. The Chief of Staff came over to me and said, "Chef Ronnie, who is the new intern?"

"Those three over there," I reluctantly replied. "Linda, Mary, and Helen."

"Which one is from Arkansas?" The Chief asked as he eyed them all.

"Mary," I answered.

"Have Mary bring the President a roast beef sandwich. Make

sure it's the one he likes with pickles, lettuce, tomatoes, and Dijon mustard on a croissant bun. Make sure it goes directly from her to him."

I called Mary to come over and talk to me.

"Mary, you have something to do," I instructed her. "You have to go see the President."

Mary was stunned. "The President?" She gasped. "Why do I have to go see him?"

"Take the sandwich we're going to make and you give it to the President. Don't hand it off to anyone or leave without delivering it directly to him. Stay until the President dismisses you."

I was told that the President invited her to a room inside the building. I don't know anything that happened except she came back later with two of the buttons on her jacket out of place. She would not tell what happened, and she wasn't smiling.

I think one of the reasons I survived this sort of turmoil going on was because I listened more than I talked. I didn't ask this girl one thing about her experience, and she went on working. I saw many, many things worse than this, but it was not my place to question or judge the President of the United States. He's my boss, but he has to sleep with himself and answer to God.

CHAPTER EIGHT
More Famous Guests

Barbara Streisand was a big fan of Bill Clinton, so she came to the White House as did many other famous stars, but Martha Stewart came to the White House because she and Hillary Clinton were like two peas in a pod. They were like sisters giggling and talking. Martha would come down to the kitchen and cook with us. She's a wonderful cook, which is why she's so famous. We were delighted when famous chefs graced our kitchen. We didn't get exposed too much to those working outside the White House, so it was always a treat for them to come visit. Bobby Flay, who is a chef out of New York came a few times as did Emeril Lagasse. The Clintons liked Chef Lagasse because of his TV program.

Sports figures seemed to be President Clinton's favorite guests. I've already talked about the big basketball sports party, but football players came by as well. Joe Namath visited along with Mike Ditka and many other football players.

Shaquille O'Neal visited with Dennis Rodman. Dennis displayed his collection of tattoos with the rings in his nose and ears. He played a little basketball with the President. During their scrimmage, Dennis knocked the President down. The Secret Service warned Mr. Rodman that he couldn't be knocking down the President, but Mr. Clinton was cordial about it.

I was very privileged to be able to serve food when these guests were here and although the Secret Service wouldn't let us approach the guests, many times they would come over and talk to us. Michael Jordan did that when I brought food up to him. I got to shake his hand and talk a little about his career. He was a gentleman and seemed more interested in my career, and I was surprised he would even be interested. Many people are interested in what goes on behind the scenes the public doesn't see, and Michael had a little of that curiosity in him.

Oprah Winfrey came, and it was one of the highlights I had as chef at the White House. I got to meet her, and she's not just somebody; she is one of the most recognized faces on the planet even back then when the Clintons were in office. That meeting led to her becoming one of my sponsors for the culinary school I am building for kids in New Orleans.

CHAPTER NINE
Chelsea Clinton

Chelsea is the only child of Bill and Hillary Clinton. She was a bubbly young lady with long reddish hair. Her only flaw was a little problem with acne, but that eventually cleared up. Chelsea respected the entire staff at the White House and especially the kitchen staff. One of the Head Chefs spent a lot of time teaching her to cook as she began to grow up. Children change a lot in eight years.

Chelsea never used her title as the daughter of the President and First Lady of the United States of America. She was never demanding, her requests were modest, and she seemed sensitive to the fact that she could have whatever she desired, but not once did she play that card. For that reason, she was loved by all my staff.

Chelsea loved grilled cheese sandwiches with a big dill pickle on the side. She loved fresh fruit punch, so we made it fresh for her whenever she came to the kitchen. She really like ginger snaps, so we kept a fresh supply for her, but her favorite meal was spaghetti with meat sauce and a side of fresh buttered corn. She always wanted a soft dinner roll with her meal, and I will never forget her favorite drink was 7-UP with cherry juice.

When Cherry 7-UP came on the market in two liter bottles, the President wouldn't allow us to give it to her. Instead, he wanted his daughter to have fresh cherry juice in the 7-Up, so we put it in fresh. I don't think Chelsea would have ever asked us to do that; even though, the fresh juice was much better than the flavored Cherry 7-UP the manufacturer put in their drinks.

Chelsea had a lot of friends, and she would invite them over for "sleepovers." We would make pizzas for the girls and then in the morning, we would treat them with Mickey Mouse pancakes for breakfast, which was the whole face of Mickey with his big ears. The girls loved those pancakes.

Something else Chelsea and her friends loved was pig-in-the-blanket, or little sausages with crescent rolls wrapped around them. We would make them Rice Krispy's treats with butter and marshmallows melted together, and then we would put M&M's in them.

I once heard one of Chelsea's most impressed friends say: "Chelsea can sure throw a party!"

Chelsea never broke up things or had selfish fits like some spoiled children do. She took on the personality of the President more than she emulated the First Lady. In fact, she was daddy's little girl.

I remember two events where Chelsea was going to school to get a special award, and the President went to the school to see his daughter get the award. In front of the entire student body and all the teachers, President Clinton gave his daughter a kiss on her forehead. No one had ever seen the President display emotion quite like that. There wasn't a dry eye in the place.

This event was a powerful lesson to me. Mrs. Clinton did not show up at this event; Chelsea's dad was there. I never stayed away when one of my eight kids was being honored at school, and learned this lesson from the most famous dad of them all.

CHAPTER TEN
Vice President Al Gore and Tipper

When Al Gore became the Vice President with President Clinton, there wasn't a problem that we needed to get to know him like we never heard of him. Vice President Gore was a long time Senator, so we had seen him around but didn't know him up close.

When Mr. Gore was sworn in as the Vice President, he scheduled a consultation with the head chefs to talk about his family and their needs. People think Al Gore was stiff and nerdy, but he was nothing like that. He was a Vice President that never tried to shine over the President, and the President and he got along extremely well and were very close friends.

Vice President Gore was different because he had different aspirations that didn't interfere with the agenda of President Clinton. Mr. Gore was going green, and he didn't make any bones about it. He got into global warming, and he wanted to save the planet.

Mr. Gore believed in healthy eating, and he was different to cook for. He was into bicycling. He could really ride. I was invited to ride with him one day, and I finally had to tell him I'd had it. I just couldn't go any more at the speed he was riding. I backed off and rode with the Secret Service back in the pack where those guys weren't trying to keep up with Al Gore and the Secret Service guys who were in shape to ride with him.

Since I was in Kitchen 2, I was with the Vice President most of the time because we did all the cooking for his family and him.

The Vice President has a beautiful home not too far from the White House. He can choose where he wants to eat. We cooked for him at his house if they were dining there, and every breakfast was made in the Vice President's home.

Mr. Gore ate all of his lunches at the White House, and dinner could be either way depending on how busy he was. Being a family man, he would bring his family to the White House if he was having dinner there, but most of the time, he ate at home.

I saw Vice President Gore every day, so I got to know him well. No all the Vice Presidents went to the White House every day, but Mr. Gore did. I also got to know Tipper Gore very well. She was a soft-spoken lady, very congenial, very nurturing, and very polite. She reminded me of a younger Barbara Bush.

Mrs. Gore was never too busy. She took time to meet and spend time with our wives and children. She never forgot their birthdays, and she sent books as presents for them to read at Christmastime. She didn't forget our anniversaries. Ann would get a bouquet of roses from Mrs. Gore for every year we were married.

Mrs. Gore was never overbearing, but she did have some special things she wanted made that she liked to eat. Cucumbers were always in her salads with our homemade croutons on top of the balsamic vinaigrette dressing. She loved avocados and grilled shrimp. The shrimp had to be grilled and not fixed any other way, and she was definitely into seafood and very little red meat although she would occasional have a steak. Some of her favorite seafood that we made for her were salmon, halibut, crab, and lobster.

One day, I introduced her to crawfish. She had no idea they even existed much less that people actually ate them. I enticed her to try some by telling her they were just "little-bitty cousins of lobsters." I made a dish I called "Crawfish Monica." She loved it so much that she had us bring it into the White House and put it on the President's menu.

Their children liked to come into the kitchen and make cookies as all the children and grandchildren of the Presidents did, and we baked a lot of cookies and birthday cakes down there in the White House kitchens. The Gores liked to have birthday parties not only for their families but for other people as well. Sometimes they would find a family that had fallen on hard times or had a death in the family. They would invite them to the White House and throw a party for them like they'd never seen before.

Mrs. Gore was a leader in helping the underprivileged in the community. She did a lot for the "Make A Wish Foundation." If an underprivileged child wanted to meet the President and Tipper could make it possible, she would. She asked the chefs to volunteer to work in the community, and I was always involved with her projects. I would go out and cook for women's abuse centers and drug abuse centers. We visited autistic kids and taught them how to cook. It was one of the most wonderful experiences of my life and career.

Four of the five First Ladies were involved with the community and worked us into their programs, but Hillary Clinton was not of that nature. If she was involved with humanitarian community projects, I didn't know about them. Through the efforts of the First Ladies of the White House, I developed a healthy respect for them. Mrs. Hillary Clinton was the hardest one to deal with and to respect.

CHAPTER ELEVEN
The Impeachment

The word was out that President Clinton was going to be impeached because of the Monica Lewinsky affair. The word also said that Mrs. Clinton was on a quest to keep her husband from being impeached. I got involved when Mrs. Clinton wanted to have a meeting.

All the supervisors were asked to prepare food for the event. Only the supervisors could prepare food for a meeting like this one. We made all types of sandwiches, cookies, and made Margaritas and Sangrias to drink and brought them to the conference room where Mrs. Clinton staged the meeting.

The whole place looked like a campaign strategy was going on. All around the room were posters with the names of certain Senators and Congressmen and Congresswomen that Mr. Clinton had fastened to the walls. Underneath the posters fashioned like a family tree was the description of things that she had found out or knew about those individuals that could harm them if ever found out.

The Secret Service was in the room along with the FBI and the CIA. They were coming up with dirt on everybody and the more they dug, the worse it got. Every person that Hillary knew had skeletons in their closets was hanging on that wall.

My crew was bringing in the food, and I told them to get out of there as quickly as possible because the less we knew about all this happening the better it would be for us. As I was leaving, Mrs. Clinton called over to me and told me that I could not leave the kitchen. She said they would be there until at least two o'clock in the morning.

"We need you to send up food as we need it," she explained.

"Mrs. Clinton, I have a sick child at home," I replied.

"We'll get somebody to go check on your child," she said.

"No, no, no ma'am. If I can't leave, you can have my keys."

"Okay," she said. "Make sure you leave somebody down there."

The next morning, I had to report to the First Lady. I went up to see her, and she did ask me how my child was doing and then she dropped a bombshell on me.

"We're going to be working every night for the next seven days. This is what I'd like for you to have ready."

She gave me different types of food to make. She had thought it all out because every item she asked for would not require a knife and fork to eat. We made pizzas, sandwiches, burritos, fish, beef, and chicken tacos. Every thing went smoothly all week.

We fed the Secret Service on the side, and they would tell us stuff that was known on the inside. The word was the First Lady had a serious conversation with every Senator and every Congressman she had dirt on and told them that if they voted to kick her husband out of office, she would expose every one of them.

Things got tough, but the First Lady had a measure of control and made sure her husband stayed in office. The President's impeachment didn't go through, and all the people close who worked with her believe she is the reason that it didn't.

I knew back then that she was going to run for President. She manipulated and put up with too much from her husband not to have that idea in the back of her mind.

The Clintons were involved in a lot of scandals that chased them into the White House, and a lot of unanswered questions that still remain. We talked about this stuff all the time in the kitchens and during our down time. We wanted to know the people we were dealing with just like the public does, and there are things we know the public does not.

Lots of people came to the White House and slept in the Lincoln bedroom because Hillary has a lot of strong connections that back her financially. I didn't know what she would do with all of those resources, but I had seen enough. She was no doubt the most devious, hardest, and meanest lady I ever worked for. I hope I never have to meet and work for a person like Mrs. Clinton ever again.

I may meet her again and when I do see her, I will give her the respect as the former First Lady, Senator, and Secretary of State; hopefully, for the sake of this country not as the President of the United States of America.

CHAPTER TWELVE
President Bill Clinton's Favorite Meals
How He Liked to Dress

Breakfast

President Clinton was a big eater. He liked his pancakes covered with sweet strawberries sent in from Ponchatoula, Louisiana. Maple Syrup from Vermont covered the strawberries, and then sliced bananas were mixed in. The pancakes were sprinkled with powdered sugar made from regular sugar that was ground to powder in a blender. He was served two Jimmy Dean spicy pork patties, and a French croissant cut in half with honey butter. Pineapple juice had to be pulp free, and the coffee with cream had three cubes of sugar added.

Lunch

Fried chicken was the President's favorite. He had three pieces on the plate, which were a breast, leg, and thigh. He would tell friends they represented the body parts of a woman. The fried chicken lunch wasn't complete without mashed potatoes with 2 tablespoons of butter, 1 ounce of chicken gravy, French style string beans cooked with olive oil, cracked pepper, and garlic. The salad was Romaine lettuce, grilled chicken, shredded Mozzarella cheese, and cracked peppercorn in a ranch buttermilk dressing with garlic croutons on top. President Clinton wanted chicken noodle soup with his lunch and topped it off with a piece of homemade pecan pie with a dob of whipped cream on top for dessert, and lemonade to drink.

Fast Foods

President Clinton was a fried chicken eater. He loved our home-made fried chicken, but he had a special pallet for KFC original with mashed potatoes and brown gravy and only dark meat because he liked African American Women, corn on the cob, and he would dab the biscuit in the gravy.

He drank 1 bottle or can of Pepsi with the meal.

Favorite Alcoholic Beverage

President Clinton drank everything. He even drank moonshine. Some friend of his sent him a jug, and he drank it.

The Pets Ate Well at the White House

The pets of the President's ate well. The Presidents had pets whether dogs and cats or both. The dogs did not eat dog food, nor were the cats were eating cat food. All the food was prepared for the pets in the kitchen. We cooked the food the dogs and cats ate, and they ate well.

The dogs didn't eat a lot of red meat, but they did gorge themselves on sautéed liver. We made chicken in various ways just like humans eat. We grilled chicken, we smoked chicken, and we would chop it up. We did not fry chicken because of the grease and fat. Barbara Bush liked to feed her dogs southern grits with the chicken.

The reasons for mentioning the pet food in this section is because of the special attention that Socks (the Clinton's cat) received in the pet menu. Mrs. Clinton demanded sardines for the cat. These were special sardines that had to be sealed in oil instead of water. The sardines also had to be the kind and brand with the heads removed. It was as if the cat would not eat a sardine with a head.

The most bizarre food we made for a pet was the liver foie gras. It is sold at some of the most expensive restaurants in the world, but we imported it at fifty dollars an ounce. It is the liver of a duck or goose that has been specially fattened. Socks didn't eat this liver every day but when he did, he loved it, and nothing was left in the dish.

The pets are under White House protection, so the Secret Service walk them every day. The only time you would see a President or First Lady walking a pet would be for photo opportunities. If the pets could not get exercise, they would put them on a treadmill.

The pets had a bath most days, and they were pampered with painted toe nails and super grooming. Some of the pets liked a massage, and they made regular visits to the pet Psychiatrist for evaluation to make sure they were performing correctly.

How He Dressed

President Clinton dressed down following a trend set by President Jimmy Carter when he shocked the America by wearing a cardigan sweater to meet with the citizens of the United States by television.

The President wore blue jeans with a shirt sporting different universities. He wore golf shorts, tank tops, sandals, tennis shoes, deck shoes, and sunglasses.

★ ★ ★ ★ ★

CLINTON

—— *Menu* ——

•

GERMAN POTATO SALAD
prepared with fresh minced garlic, sliced green onions
and Dijon mustard

BBQ BABY BACK RIBS
with fresh watermelon bbq sauce,
served with four cheese baked macaroni

TRADITIONAL RAISIN BREAD PUDDING
with house-made custard,
all topped with a rum sauce glaze

———— • ————

PREPARATIONS FOR THREE PEOPLE

SALAD

6 medium size red skinned potatoes
¼ cup red wine vinegar
1 tbsp onion powder
1 tbsp minced garlic
3 white onions
3 green onions
3 tbsp Dijon mustard
½ lemon
Salt to taste
Red pepper to taste

DIRECTIONS

1) Skin half of each potato and cut into quarters. Boil w/ salt and red pepper for 18 min. Remove and pat dry. Place in bowl.

2) Combine additional ingredients in bowl (juice half lemon). Whisk together.

3) Add potatoes and toss together.

4) Serve.

ENTRÉE

12 ribs (4 per person)
1 watermelon
½ cup brown sugar
½ cup ketchup
¼ cup yellow mustard
1 tbsp cumin
1 tsp garlic powder
1 tsp onion powder
1 tsp red pepper flakes

1 tsp oregano
Salt to taste
8 oz penne pasta macaroni
2 oz feta cheese
2 oz cheddar cheese
2 oz Gouda cheese
2 oz pepper jack cheese
½ cup heavy whipping cream
3 raw eggs (room temp)
2 tsp white pepper
¾ cup breadcrumbs
½ stick unsalted butter
2 bunches mustard greens
4 cups chicken broth
1 onion (diced)
½ bell pepper (diced)
2 ribs celery (diced)
2 cloves garlic (mashed)
2 smoked ham hocks

DIRECTIONS

BBQ Baby Back Ribs

1) Wash ribs, remove membrane on back of ribs. Dry rub creole seasoning, wrap in three layers aluminum foil. Place ribs on sheet pan, put in oven at 425 degrees for 50 min.

2) While ribs are cooking, make BBQ sauce.

   a. Slice watermelon in half, remove seeds, blend watermelon meat until liquid, strain and save liquid.

   b. In pot, add watermelon juice, brown sugar, ketchup, yellow mustard, cumin, garlic powder, onion powder, red pepper flakes, oregano, and salt to taste. Turn on medium heat, stirring occasionally. Reduce by half.

3) Serve w/ macaroni and cheese.

Four Cheese Baked Macaroni

1) Cook pasta according to package.

2) Place pasta in bowl, break up eggs and mix, add 4 cheeses, heavy whipping cream, and pepper, pour macaroni and cheese into 9" x 13" pan, sprinkle top w/ bread crumbs.

3) Put macaroni and cheese in oven at 350 degrees for 35 min. or until golden brown.

4) Soak mustard greens in water and allow dirt/residue to sink to bottom. Remove greens and pat dry. Season on smoked ham hock.

5) Cook ham hock on stove at medium heat w/ diced onion, bell peppers, and celery. Add mashed garlic, red pepper to taste. Cook 40 minutes w/ lid. Check hock for tenderness, remove skin and fat, take meat off bone and return to greens.

6) Serve w/ ribs.

DESSERT

1 loaf raisin bread (remove crust)
1 cup whole milk
2 cups heavy whipping cream
1 cup white sugar
4 tbsp vanilla
1 tbsp cinnamon
1 cup light brown sugar
1 stick melted butter
2 eggs
½ cup golden raisins
¼ cup rum

DIRECTIONS

1) Toast bread on sheet pan in oven at 325 degrees ~10 min.

2) For custard, mix whole milk, 1 cup heavy whipping cream, white sugar, 1 tbsp vanilla, cinnamon, 1 stick melted butter, 2 whipped eggs, in one bowl.

3) Spray 9" x 13" pan with oil, place bread pudding in pan, cover with custard mix. Sprinkle raisins over all.

4) Place 9 " x 13" pan in larger pan w/ ½" water (bread will not burn), place in oven 4 min at 350 degrees.

5) In separate pot, add 1 cup heavy whipping cream, 2 tbsp vanilla, 1 cup light brown sugar. Place on stove at medium heat, stir until sugar dissolves. Add rum of choice, cook 10 min. Glaze over bread pudding.

6) Garnish pudding w/ pecans or walnuts.

7) Serve.

SECTION 4
PRESIDENT GEORGE W. BUSH

CHAPTER ONE
Very Difficult Presidency

George W. Bush became President after a very controversial election. We all remember the "Hanging Chads" that decided the election down in Florida. I went through the same thing every time we changed Presidents. Would I or wouldn't I be retained at my job? I loved being a White House Chef, and the thought of changes would get my stomach all messed up and my sleeping habits. It was a gut wrenching experience.

I knew President George W. Bush well because of all the visits he made when his father was President. I had a very amicable relationship with him, so it was sort of like a homecoming. We all welcomed the former Governor of Texas and got ready for his tenure in the White House as President. Laura Bush had that beautiful smile that made you love her. The President introduced Vice President Dick Cheney.

When Laura Bush visited Kitchen 2, she decided to retain everybody in there, so I was safe again for the time being. In fact, there were only two chefs that got relieved, and they were both in Kitchen 1. The word was on the floor that President Bush fired them. We heard it was because of some direct criticism. They were Democrats and made the mistake of mixing their politics with cooking food. This wasn't the first time this happened. You have to keep your mouth shut around the work environment because news travels at lightning speed.

All the anxiety had no foundation because the Bush's kept me in my Kitchen 2, and I would work for the new Vice President

Dick Cheney. The eight years I spent working with President Bush were the most difficult of the all the years I spent there, and Vice President Cheney didn't make things any better.

There were many things that made life difficult during this Administration. President Bush was noticeably stressed all the time, and he was aging quickly. The wars were weighing on him. I realized how much the Presidents suffer when our boys are being killed over senseless conflicts that seemingly can't be avoided. Sons and daughters were dying all the time, and the papers were publishing lists every day of those who were tragically killed.

The President was greatly misunderstood. He couldn't express himself very well and when he would go on TV to report to America, they didn't take him serious that he was actually on top of everything going on and in charge of his world. He didn't always look Presidential when he was talking to America.

We watched the news on TV just like everybody else did in America. When the President left the country, we would keep up with what was going on because we knew by the inside information coming in and out of the kitchens the peril that the United States was in a lot of the time. We also felt the George W. Bush Presidency would be a rocky one.

The first incident happened one day while we were watching the President on the news during a press conference with the Iraqi's. Suddenly a guy named Muntadhar al-Zaidi took off his shoe and threw it at the President. This is the ultimate insult you give to a person, and he called him a "dog."

Mrs. Bush was in her office watching the conference, and she put in a call to the Secret Service where he was overseas and told them to get her husband out of there. If you watch the news, you will see the Secret Service grab the President by both arms and got him to safety. They were going to kill the President on television for the whole world to see.

The President was scrutinized and dragged through hell with the media tracking him and dogging him every day. It wasn't long until you could see the toll it was taking on him and Mrs. Bush.

I was put on duty to take food to the airport on a direct order from Mrs. Bush. We were feeding the family members who were waiting on the bodies of their sons and daughters that were killed in the war. Those memories will haunt me until the day I die.

When the plane landed, everybody stood at attention. It was an emotional scene to see a row of black limousine hearses pulling up to retrieve the dead bodies of these heroic soldiers. The Honor Guard went up to the plane and removed twenty-one caskets, and then the twenty-one guns salute. The firing in perfect unison, and the pop, pop, pop sound of the guns firing brought back tearful memories for me of Vietnam.

I thought about how my son could be one of those boys. I also would have given my life if one of those soldier boys could have been saved. These thoughts ran all through me. This was a different kind of duty I was experiencing as a chef. A guy standing near me asked why I was crying?

I said, "Why not? That could have been my child."

This war was going to be on the whole eight years of George W. Bush's Presidency. At the time, I didn't think much about the toll it was going to take on me. Working for President Bush was one of the hardest things I was ever going to do. He was misunderstood in my opinion, but I got along with him with no problems. I like him, but he had some habits the public wasn't aware of until after his term was concluded.

President Bush drank a lot of whiskey. He loved Bourbon and beer. The rumor was he smoked marijuana. He would get tipsy, and Mrs. Bush was working as hard as she could to keep him straight. You see all this when you are working in the presence of these people. We would see marijuana roaches when we went in to clean to take the plates and silverware back to the kitchen. I didn't personally do the cleaning, but my crew would come back and ask, "What's going on here?" I was sad for him. I thought, *what a waste.*

There's a lot of pressure for me not to tell these things, but this is how I lived as a chef in the White House. We never said anything to anyone, and the Secret Service would tell us to keep our mouths shut, and we did.

He was not much of a womanizer, but I do know of one affair he had that was very brief, but it happened. We were preparing a dinner for a late meeting. After it was over, only the President and Dr. Condoleezza Rice were left in the room. We were told that there was a brief affair and after First Lady Laura Bush found out about it, she told the President if it ever happened again, she would cut it off. She also told Dr. Rice she needed to think about leaving her post.

Dr. Rice was a well-respected intelligent lady. It was difficult to think that she would get involved like that, but we were told they were drinking wine and one thing led to another. As far as I know, nothing every happened again with the President like that.

I had issues with the President. My oldest son was sent to the war and was wounded in action twice. I was distressed over this, so I waited until one day I would take some food to his office, and my plan was to confront President Bush as to why he sent my son to war.

I entered the President's office with food. "Why did you send my son to war, Mr. President?"

"I will look into it, Chef," he said.

He never did look into it as far as I know because nothing changed until Mrs. Bush got involved. My son got shot up, and I was able to go visit him the first time. They sent him back, and he got shot again in the arm and leg.

When Mrs. Bush found out this happened again, she got my son transferred out of Afghanistan. The Army sent him to Germany, so he was with his wife and three children. To this day, Laura Bush has not forgotten what she did for me.

I got to cook more for the President than I had the others I worked for. President Bush liked Mexican food, and I was an expert at making those special dishes. I also cooked for Mrs. Bush and her family when they would come over. I developed a strong relationship with her that continues to this day.

CHAPTER TWO
9/11
The Day Never Forgotten

No American alive today who experienced that fateful day on September 11, 2001 will ever forget where they were when a foreign enemy attacked the United States on our soil. I can never forget the horror that took place that day and to be in the White House while it was happening was the most unnerving experience I ever had since my Vietnam War days as a POW.

President Bush was out of town that day. I was in the kitchen when someone yelled to us that the President was on television. We quickly flipped the channel to see what was up, and the President was talking with some children. Suddenly, the Secret Service whispered in his ear, and the President immediately left his meeting. The news feed started, and we knew they had taken the President away for safety.

Soon we learned that the Pentagon had been hit, and that another plane was presumably heading for the White House but had been taken down by passengers on the plane.

CHAPTER THREE
Laura Bush

First Lady Laura Bush was just that. She was a First Lady in everything she did. She was a schoolteacher, librarian, and she was dedicated to reading and learning. Her first initiative was to influence children to read. She spent a lot of time and involved herself in a lot of programs that focused on children reading.

Because of Laura Bush, "No Child Left Behind" became a reality. The No Child Left Behind Law ensures that no child will be left sitting in a classroom without being taught and given the opportunity to learn.

President Bush also increased the laws for IEP's and 504's. Individualized Education Program is mandated by the IDEA (Individuals with Disabilities Education Act). In my opinion, this was President George W. Bush and Laura Bush's greatest contribution during their Presidency.

The 504 Section of the Rehabilitation Act specifies that no child with a disability can be excluded from a federally funded program. This includes activities for elementary, secondary, and postsecondary schooling. The law defines "disability" as a physical or mental impairment that substantially limits a person's life activities. Physical impairments, injuries, and chronic diseases are included. The main part of this law is its protection of persons with learning disabilities. Devices are provided to these disabled kids free of charge, so that they have the same opportunity to perform activities at or near the level of their peers.

My last child is the beneficiary of what Laura Bush brought

to this country. She worked closer with her husband than any of the First Ladies. She was involved and because of her untiring service, my child got a chance to function a normal life. Mrs. Bush would walk around the White House involving herself daily in what few others would not or could not do. She instructed her staff to correct all the wrong things that she realized were deterrents that create a negative workplace. She fixed everything she could possibly find.

The First Lady took the time to talk to the staff. She wanted to know them but more importantly, she wanted to know what our needs were and our personal concerns. If we had a need, we would tell Mrs. Bush, and she would make it happen. She took care of her twin daughters, Jenna and Barbara, by making sure they got a proper education and were working toward college.

Laura Bush was a great First Lady in the sense that she involved herself with her family. She invited her in-laws to visit and have a lunch or dinner, and other people were always coming by to visit. She welcomed them all.

Some of the family would get a little wild sometimes. There would be sleepovers, so we had to do the cooking. We would deliver pizzas and in the mornings, we would deliver breakfast of Belgium waffles, pancakes, omelet stations, cut up cantaloupes, honeydew melons, pineapples, and put them into watermelon halves.

The parties with the families and friends would sometimes get a little wild. One the guests brought an inappropriate movie, and Laura Bush found out about it. She got it out of there, and no one knows what happened to it. When she popped in on them, they straightened up quickly. The worse thing that happened was occasionally something antique that had been around for along time would get broken.

People ask me all the time how the twins treated me. They had their own parties about once a month with friends coming and especially from college. Mrs. Bush kept as tight a reign on them as possible, but they could get wild when she wasn't around. They never smart mouthed any of the staff, and they definitely never talked back to their parents. It was like their dad wasn't the President of the United States, and their mom wasn't the First Lady. I attribute this to the way Laura Bush brought them up during the Presidency.

Even though the girls were typical teenagers, they didn't run all over the White House sleeping in every room. They had their own rooms and stuck to them. They did love showing off the White House to their friends, but who wouldn't be enamored with friends that were daughters of a United States President? It was fun listening to them tell their versions of how things were the way they were, and how they got to be that way.

Laura Bush loves her husband dearly, and she stands by him. In fact, her favorite song was *Stand by Your Man* by Tammy Wynette and later made a greater song by Candi Staton. Mrs. Bush played the song every time the President left the White House for a trip.

When President Bush traveled to New York after the tragic 9-11 terrorist bombing, Mrs. Bush was concerned the terrorist cell was still operating in the country and would do even more damage. She told President Bush before he went up there that this wasn't a political showdown. People lost their lives because we weren't conscientious enough to prevent something like this from happening. She had a lot of influence concerning the President's decisions on many things, but this event rocked the Country and affected the President.

Laura Bush told us that the President was suffering an abnormal amount of pain over the 9-11 situation. He knew there were terrorists operating and plotting to attack the United States on its own soil. He put other people in charge and made it their responsibility, and nothing got done. Both the President and the First Lady suffered a lot of emotional pain that the public didn't realize.

Mrs. Bush was also like her mother-in-law Mrs. Barbara Bush. Barbara Bush would go visit your kids, and so would Laura Bush. She loved Dr. Seuss, so she would bring his storybooks and give them to the children.

Laura Bush would show up at the annual Easter egg hunts we put on for the families of the White House. The children became involved with her at the first egg hunt the Bush's had when President Bush came on board. Mrs. Bush showed up in a pantsuit and jumped into a bag with one leg and did the sack race. She did the egg toss, the egg race, and the three-legged race. She did all these things with the children, and they loved her for it.

First Lady Laura Bush loved certain foods I made for her. Her favorite was carrot soufflé. Most people never heard of this dish, but it was made famous by Piccadilly. You make it by boiling down carrots and adding powdered sugar, white pepper, eggs, heavy cream, and turn this into a pudding. You then bake the concoction in the oven. Once it's finish baking, you sprinkle powered sugar on top. You can trick people into thinking you've made a sweet potato dish. Piccadilly sells carrot soufflé every day of the year.

Mrs. Bush really liked lamb chops. She ate her chops with some mint jelly, and she wanted nine different vegetables with it. She wanted no pasta or potatoes. With this meal, she drank sweet tea with no lemon.

Without any hesitation, I will tell you that I loved Laura Bush more than any of the First Ladies. Not that Nancy Reagan, Barbara Bush, or Michelle Obama were not wonderful to work for, but Laura Bush connected with me from the get go, and I absolutely adored her. She and I were close and still are while this book is being written, and the story's being told. If Laura Bush would run for President, I would be her number one campaigner.

CHAPTER FOUR
Vice President Dick Cheney

Dick Cheney was the Vice President I worked with, who I never liked or respected very much. He was a mean son-of-a-bitch and an asshole. He's upside any bad adjective you want to attribute to him. They would all be accurate, so pick one. He's the only elected official I worked with, who took his title and abused it.

He cursed out the President on a daily basis. It got so bad that they would call the Senior President Bush and ask him to come over to the White House to calm things down. As soon as President Bush, Sr. would leave, Dick Cheney would come right back in rare form.

One day, Dick Cheney told President George W. Bush, while all the senior chefs were in his presence and could hear him clearly,

"I run this goddamn White House, not you! You do what I tell you to do and nothing else!"

When President Bush was flying around in the presidential plane, Air Force One, while the threat of attack on his life was happening during 9/11, Vice President Cheney took over running the White House. Dick Cheney took charge.

Dick Cheney made it clear to all of us that he was indeed in charge.

"President Bush is not here, and I am in control of the country," he told us. "You don't question my authority. Understand?"

We didn't question him because he had power and a lot of it.

He could whisk us so far away from the duties we performed at the White House that no one would ever hear of us again. I respected his authority only because I was afraid of him as everyone was. He abused his office. We didn't know at the time that the President has to be viably proven to be dead before the Vice President is in charge of running the Government of the United States.

Vice President Cheney set up a command post in the basement of the White House as the safest place to be in case another plane would be heading toward the White House. From there, he started giving his commands. He kept one hundred percent track of where the President was at all times. He was tracking the fire and police departments and gathering information when he found out a plane was heading for the White House but instead hit the Pentagon.

The Vice President developed some very strange habits during his tenure of "running the house." We learned from our inside informants that the Vice President was wired up and recording everything you said to him. His Secret Service personnel were like the Gestapo, watching everything that was moving in and out of the White House.

He roughed people up that got in his way and was establishing himself as an authority to be reckoned with if you ever crossed a line he didn't want crossed. When Vice President Cheney went on that famous hunting trip where he accidentally shot his buddy, some of the White House staff believed he "accidentally shot the guy on purpose."

I was Dick Cheney's personal chef, and I cooked the food he wanted anytime he wanted it. He had a very bad heart because he was a chain smoker since he was a teenager. He had surgery, and that created a huge change in his diet. It also made him become abusive.

He began a routine that wasn't a routine at all. I never knew when he was going to make a demand that I make him some food. He wanted me to work extremely late and when I complained that I had a family at home that needed to see me, he would get visibly upset. Respectful of the consequences of being left on the street without a means to support my family, I would back down. I called my wife, Anne, many times and explained my situation, and that I would be coming in late that night or not at all. She would be upset but would always say, "Okay."

I would cook some food and have the Secret Service deliver it to my house. It was during this time that I felt I needed to get out of there. The Vice President would yell at my staff and disrespect them. He yelled at the chefs under me, but he never hollered at me. I don't know why he didn't, but he avoided screaming at me about things he was upset about. Maybe he was afraid I would leave because by this time, I knew a lot and was aware of a lot.

He abused Kitchen 2. He would purposely wait until the last minute when we were wrapping up and going home to place a "special" order that would keep us on call until he was served. This habit became exceptionally irritating, frustrating, and depressing. I wanted to get out of that place so badly that sometimes it would make me cry the stress was so awful.

I need to be fair, though. He did not directly treat me rudely or embarrass me in front of the others like he would do so often do to the others in front of me. Maybe he was trying to send me a message of some kind that would keep me in his grasp. Maybe this is how he thought he could control me. He made me work late hours, and I did them. I didn't work all those hours because I was afraid of him. I did it because I wanted the others to have the freedom to go home and be with their families.

Honestly, the Vice President couldn't *make* me do anything I didn't want to do. I respected the office and had sworn an oath that I took seriously to uphold. It had always been my modus operandi to be the last to leave and the first to arrive. Pleasing Vice President Cheney had nothing to do with it.

The Vice President had a ton of meetings. He had them all the time, so he ate most of his meals at the White House except on the weekends when he would eat at home. Most of the time, Mrs. Cheney would come to the White House to eat her meals with the Vice President.

My relationship with Vice President Cheney was in one word, "horrible." I always knew that if he got so unbearable I couldn't stand it anymore that I could go to the Senior Bush and get some help. He would talk to his son and Mrs. Bush, and they would put a stop to it. I almost did that a couple of times but held my peace. I also knew in the back of my mind that President George W. Bush would have a hard time confronting Vice President Cheney about anything. Laura Bush would most likely carry the torch because she was unafraid of Dick Cheney.

Vice President Cheney took advantage of President Bush's weaknesses. George W. Bush was not a seasoned politician, and Dick Cheney had been there a long time working before as President Gerald Ford's Chief of Staff. He literally knew everybody, and that gave him leverage over the unseasoned President he was working for.

The Vice President had a close relationship with President Bush, Sr., and that was also some leverage for him to dominate President George W. Bush. The President didn't have a temper, and he didn't like confrontations and hassles. He went out of his way to avoid them. About the only time you saw President Bush get upset and angry was playing sports. He didn't like to lose. The Vice President took advantage of all this. He was the controlling dictator of the President, and the President allowed it.

The relationship between the President and Vice President was disconcerting to the staff. Even some of Dick Cheney's personal staff detested his behavior much of time except for those he handpicked personally. They were rough, and some of them were former Navy Seals. They were the Gestapo. They kept the Vice President out of the way of everybody, so you could never approach him. You had to be way up the ladder before he would talk to you or give you the time of day.

The Vice President had to deal with me because I planned his meals. When I approached his office, his personal Secret Service bodyguards would make me stand there until the Vice President gave the word to let me in. The three Vice Presidents previously didn't have this kind of silliness going on all the time.

You couldn't walk in on them, but a knock on the door would get you in or if the office door was opened, you could walk on in and conduct your business in a normal fashion.

Vice President Cheney has two daughters, Liz and Mary. Liz would eventually run a campaign to be a Senator from Wyoming, and Mary is openly gay and married to a woman. Liz, publicly claimed that she believed a marriage union was between a man and a woman. I know these girls, and it surprises me that Mary ended up in a gay marriage.

Second Lady, Lynne Cheney, is an extremely intelligent woman with a Ph.D. in 19th Century British Literature. She did not take an active role in her husband's office although I believe she supported him. She was rarely around the White House opting to stay away and work on her private projects. We would only see her when we would take food over to their house. Sometimes, we didn't see her then because she would be upstairs and wouldn't come down. She would yell down to us when she wanted us to leave, and we would go.

Mrs. Cheney could be seen at some formal dinners, but no one approached her casually. She was a low-key quiet lady, and the word was that the Vice President didn't treat her very well. I can't validate this for the truth, but he was not pleasant to her when they were together.

I know people can change, and the Vice President has some major health problems that affected him greatly. Maybe he was frustrated and took it out on everybody around him. However, this book is about my observations, opinions, relationships, and how my life was as a White House Chef.

CHAPTER FIVE
Special Visitors
Knighted by the Queen

President Bush had a strong relationship with the Israelis. He supported them heavily, and I got to meet Ariel Sharon, the Prime Minister, and helped make the meal the President served. I loved meeting the Israeli leaders because of their no- nonsense approach to the business they were doing. I support Israel because outside of England, they are our strongest allies in the world.

One of the biggest thrills of my career was when I got to meet Pope Benedict. President Bush had a good relationship with him; even though, the President was a Protestant.

I got invited by the President to fly with him and help with the food on the plane. The food was not cooked on the plane back then. We made it in the kitchen, and then took it to the plane. We carried it in foil containers, and the meal is microwaved and placed on the plates. These are very small light meals that hold the entourage over while they're flying. Soups, salads, and sandwiches are made with nothing fried, and nothing that would produce gas or upset the stomach.

Bill Gates came to the White House often to visit Clinton and then George W. Bush. He gives away a lot of money, and I think some of the projects Laura Bush was involved with were funded outside the Government. Bill Gates and his wife contributed to a lot of different causes.

The Gates were among very few people who could knock on the front door unannounced and get into the White House to see a President. There were some big shot bankers that had that privilege as well.

Barbara Streisand had an open invitation and even though she was much more liberal thinking on the political side than President Bush, he was a big fan. Laura Bush likes Beyoncé, so she came a couple of times. Lady Gaga was there because of the twins.

One of the more puzzling person's that was invited to the White House by President Bush was Master P. I took the food up during that meeting, and I can't reveal what the meeting was about, but they were talking business.

The President and Mrs. Bush had a favorite set menu they would feed the stars and special private guests they entertained. We would start off with *Shrimp Round*. It was made with a toasted piece of whole wheat bread, and then cut with a cookie cutter, and aioli was put on it. The dip was make with garlic and butter with a caper in the middle and a dash of paprika. You dip shrimp in it and is really delicious.

I loved to make asparagus rolled in Kobe beef, and they loved it, too. Roast beef was wrapped around the asparagus spears and baked in the oven. I made miniature cheesecakes with a strawberry glaze and placed a strawberry on top.

Ganache muffins are made with a heavy cream and chocolate melted together and poured over the cake. We made fruit bowls with Philadelphia Cream Cheese. We shaped them like birds, fish, and turtles and the sprinkled powdered sugar on top. The President likes dolphins, so we always had a dolphin ice sculpture as the decoration. We put food coloring in the ice to make it bluish-gray – the color of a dolphin.

THE QUEEN

Queen Elizabeth II will always be the most special visitor I met while working as a White House Chef.

Mrs. Laura Bush was the one and only reason I got to cook for Queen Elizabeth when the President invited her for a State dinner. I was selected by Laura Bush to make the dessert for that dinner. One really bad thing happened during the Queen's visit that was caused by President Bush.

The Queen came to tour the United States as the guest of President Bush in April of 2008. The President made an announcement, and then tried to crack a joke that backfired. He said that Queen Elizabeth II was as old as our country. She got deeply offended and announced that she was leaving and going back to England. Laura Bush stepped in and saved the day.

My kitchen was helping with the State dinner, and I was in charge of the dessert. I was present when the Queen told Mrs. Bush that she was leaving. Mrs. Bush implored her to not leave and instead she escorted the Queen on a private tour of Washington. Mrs. Bush charmed the Queen, and she dismissed what happened as a bad joke and remained on her tour of the United States.

We ended up with the best State dinner I witnessed my entire time as a White House Chef. There were twenty-five hundred people at that dinner, so I made twenty-five hundred Crème Brule's.

Now remember I was in the Kitchen 2 at that time, and Kitchen 1 was responsible for this particular meal. They brought in celebrity chefs to take part in cooking the different courses of the dinner. The whole display that President Bush was putting forth was the brainstorm of his wife.

This was by far the greatest dinner I had been privileged to help serve. Every piece of the dinner was orchestrated to the fullest. The President came in dressed in his tux while "Hail to the Chief" was playing, and then we saw the Queen. She came in with all the regalia you could ever imagine a queen would show. She was stunning with her diamonds, sparkling crown of jewels, a sash across her dress, and escorted by the Prince.

There were four chefs working the dinner: Wolfgang Puck, Bobby Flay, Emma Lagasse, and me. The Secret Service had instructed us not to approach the Queen but if she came in our territory, we were to click our heels, bow our heads, and say, "Yes, Your Majesty."

After the meal was over, the Queen came to meet us. I was the last one in line because I served the dessert. Before she got to us, Wolfgang Puck said,

"Ronnie, don't you crack a joke on the Queen."

"Go ahead and crack a joke, Ronnie. You work at the White House, they're not going to fire you," Emma Lagasse said.

The President and Mrs. Bush accompanied the Queen as the President introduced us. When the Queen came to me, she said in her heavy British accent,

"Master Chef, do you think it's possible that I could get the recipe for your dessert?"

"Yes your Majesty," I said as I raised my eyes to meet hers, "but you don't have enough money."

"What?" The Queen asked.

President Bush looked at the others and me very quickly as if to say, *Oh Lord, we're in trouble now.*

Prince Phillip, the Duke of Edinburg, laughed because he thought it was funny.

"Your Majesty, there is a credit card called Visa." I said.

The Queen turned to the President and said, "George, what is Visa?"

"Your Majesty, can I explain before the President messes up. I don't want him saying the wrong things?" I asked lugubriously.

"That would be most appropriate," she answered.

I told her that there is a credit card that will buy a plane ticket to your country, and will buy my children's books for college. I can even buy a Dooney and Bourke purse.

"What is a Dooney and Bourke purse?" She asked.

"It's a very expensive purse that the women in America like very much," I explained. "A trip to your country to cook for you would be as priceless as the birth of one of my children."

She then looked me in the eye with a bright smile and said, "that would be most wonderful."

The Queen left me standing with that last thought and impression of the greatest Monarch on the earth.

My wife and I were building a house for my father-in-law,

so we left Washington shortly after this magnificent dinner was now a favorite memory and traveled to New Orleans.

We were there only a few days when a black Suburban pulled up at front curb of the house. The Secret Service and the FBI were in the car. It was curious because in the hands of one of the Secret Servicemen, was a tape recorder and an envelope.

"Are you Master Chef Ronnie Seaton," the Secret Serviceman said, "please show your I.D."

I pulled out my Identification and credential and showed it to him. He then told me that they had a letter they wanted me to read, and then they would tape my response. I opened the letter from President George Bush.

"I George Bush, Jr. have a directive that Master Chef Ronnie Seaton will travel to Buckingham Palace in London, England December 19 and cook the Queen's Christmas dinner. What is your response?"

Of course I accepted, so we went off to Baton Rouge where I would go from a Top Secret Clearance to a Crypto Clearance. Top Secret Clearance is the highest in our country, and Crypto Clearance is where you are going Internationally to deal with a head of state.

I got my clearance, and my two sons eight and ten years old were coming with us. Ann rejected the invitation. She started studying with the Jehovah Witnesses. When I challenged her that she is Catholic, she said she was just visiting and talking with them.

"We did a little Bible study," she said.

"Ann," I pleaded, "You can't do this."

"Why?" She asked.

"They're a Cult! They don't vote and don't believe in Government."

The FBI stood by and told her they knew where she'd been and had pictures. They asked me what I was going to do?

I turned to Ann. "I'll see you when I get back."

"No, no, no," she complained. "I'm going to England. What do I need to do?"

The FBI told her to sign a statement that all she was doing was reading with the Jehovah Witnesses, and that she is still Catholic, and then she could go.

We returned home to New Orleans where we were building a house for her father, and another car pulls up. Out stepped Bob Mackie, and he was there to fit my wife for an evening gown. Cartier Jewelers came and showed her diamonds and garnets to pick out to wear with her dress.

She was fitted with shoes, and a furrier showed up to fit her for a stole. Bill Blass came and measured the boys for clothes. An Egyptian tailor came who made linen cotton jackets and fitted the boys and me.

I went back to the White House, and I had until November to get the menu together to present for the dinner. Mary Landrieu, our Senator from Louisiana, told me I needed to take all Louisiana food. The salad, sea food soup, blood orange sorbet, lump crab meat that was served with the lamb chops, duchess potatoes, asparagus, and a chocolate pecan pie were all made or raised in Louisiana. Even the wines came from the vineyards in Louisiana.

When we arrived in England, there were ten chefs from ten different castles who came to work with me. My boys were given little white chef jackets made to their sizes, and they worked with the plates out of the kitchen.

The meal was for twenty-eight people and my wife. Being a former dancer, Ann knew exactly how to courtesy, and she had learned to sing "God Save the Queen."

After the meal had come off perfectly, I was in the kitchen. The Queen sent word for me to come up to see her. She asked me to introduce myself to her twenty-eight guests that also included her family.

I had a can of "Slap Ya Momma" Louisiana seasoning in my pocket. The Secret Service knew I was going to crack a joke on the Queen, but her guards didn't know this.

The Queen asked me to say a few words, and so I said, "I wish your mother was here today. I know she has died and gone to heaven, and she would have enjoyed this meal. The food tastes so good in Louisiana in the City of New Orleans..."

I reached in my pocket. Her guards nervously moved a step closer, and the Queen was right in front of me.

"Slap Ya Momma," I yelled.

The Prince laughed, but the Queen again didn't think my joke was funny.

"Sometimes you just wanna slap ya momma," I said to the Prince.

"Master Chef, I didn't really see this as funny," the Queen said.

"Your Majesty, this is a spice that we use on our food in Louisiana. In fact I "Slapped Ya Momma" tonight on your food, and I want to give this can to you."

The Queen looked at it and then said, "Well, I have something for you."

"What is that your Majesty?"

"Would you please kneel," she replied.

"Why do you want me to kneel, your Majesty?"

"I want to do something special for you," she replied.

My sons, Xavier and Savir were standing next to me when a Beef Eater came into the room carrying a pillow with a sword on it. Savir, who has ADHD, cringed up next to me gripping my jacket.

"Momma, the Queen is going to cut daddy's head off!"

Everyone was laughing. "Please kneel," the Queen commanded.

"Your Majesty, I can't kneel because of my wounds in the Vietnam War, but I will get down as far as I can."

"No young one," the Queen said. "I have something special for your father."

I knelt down, and the Queen lifted the gold sword about two feet long with precious stones lining the handles.

"I Queen Elizabeth the Second of Buckingham Palace of London, England dub thee Lord Master Chef Ronnie Seaton, Sr. Rise and meet your public."

I looked up at her and asked, "What did you just do?"

"I Knighted you. You are now a Knight of my realm."

"But I'm not from England, Your Majesty," I cried.

"Your meal was so impressive that I had to do this for you," she explained. "You are the only American chef I've ever knighted, and I don't regret it."

My wife raised her hand and said to the Queen, "May I ask one question?"

"Lady Ann," the Queen responded.

"What do you mean?" Ann replied.

"You have that title," the Queen said. "You are one of my ladies. What is your question?"

"I can't call my husband Lord. The Lord is God." Ann said.

"In England Knights are Lord but in America, you can call him, Sir."

"I can't call him sir," Ann replied.

"But you are Lady Ann," said the Queen.

"Then I guess I will call him Sir."

This exchange between the Queen of England and Ann Seaton was very amusing to everybody in the Hall including the Queen. I don't think she was quite ready for the folksy demeanor of these African American people from Louisiana.

I have been over to England twice since then, and they call me Lord Master Chef. There are only two Master Chefs the Queen has knighted. I am the only American, and one other is from England. I am the only Master Chef knighted, who is also a Ph.D.

When I returned to the White House, the President asked me to come to the Oval Office. He had a very special surprise for me and presented me with my second Freedom Medal.

As upset as I had been with President Bush, I began to see that he really was a good man, and I respected him much more. He was winning my confidence and faith that his decisions were based on what he really felt was best for this country, and he was trying his best to lead it in the right way.

9/11

These were eight years of hard times. I was sent to New York after the bombing to supervise the Gumbo crew who fed first responders. I saw body after body being taken out of all that rubble. I have a flag that was draped over some bodies that has bloodstains on it. It was given to me as a memory for my work. It was hard to see so many people who had been killed and so senselessly. I blamed the President for allowing so many of these dangerous foreigners in our country.

Everybody remembers where he was when the attacks took place. We were cooking in the kitchen. We have one TV in there that is really for the news. Someone said that President Bush was on television. We all looked and recognized one of the Secret Servicemen that was standing by President Bush. He was leaning over to the President's ear and telling him something. Later, we found out that he was informing the President that the World Trade Center had been bombed, and they needed to get him out of there immediately.

They put the President on Air Force One and flew him until they knew it was secure enough to get him on the ground. Mrs. Bush called down to the kitchens and told everybody not to leave but stay put. We called our families because we wanted to make sure they were safe. Soon after, we found out there was a plane heading toward the White House.

The Vice President was secured in a special area, and we were all ordered to the basement. Vice President Cheney then took charge, and we didn't know what that meant at the time, but we found out.

The President had the "football" with him. That is a briefcase with all the codes for nuclear attacks. Vice President Cheney went crazy. He started hollering at people and started throwing stuff, and then the Chief of Staff told us to start making coffee and sandwiches.

People ask me all the time if I was scared. I was beyond scared; I was terrified, and I didn't know if I would ever see my family again. We were making sandwiches in the basement that is really a bomb shelter.

We did not have television in the shelter, but we had radios, and we listened to the news and the events that were taking place. We were in the basement over twelve hours while the Secret Service made sure everything was well secured to protect us. No one knew what was going to happen and when the Pentagon was hit just down the road, we froze. There wasn't a person in there, who wasn't trembling. I'd been in the war and captured by the Viet Cong, but I was never more fearful than when I was locked in that basement.

When it was time to go, the Secret Service came down and asked me to count all my people and make sure they were all accounted for. When they were, they let them go home. I told my staff to stay close to their phones and do not leave town. It was funny, but they were more worried about whether they would get paid than they were about the terrorists on the loose killing people. I told them they would get paid if I had to pay them myself. People are strange sometimes.

The Secret Service brought about fifty thousand dollars in cash and gave the crew money. This was extraordinary because nobody knew the computers were broken and out of commission, and they didn't want the staff left with no resources to feed their families. I thought about this for a very long time. Somebody ordered this to take place because the Secret Service doesn't have access to money like that nor can they make a decision like that on their own. Cash was brought down and distributed because everyone knew banks were closed and almost certainly there would be no access to the ATM machines. They didn't want the kitchen staff left without money.

I found out that one of my buddies was in the Twin Tower when it was hit. He worked with me in the White House Kitchen. He was dismissed when President Clinton came on board and took a job as the head chef in one of the restaurants in the World Trade Center. He was Jonathon Smith, and he worked for the Four Seasons. I was the person who called his wife and told her that her husband was killed. It was a bad day and one of the worst in my life.

Vice President Cheney let us leave the basement, and I went to the kitchen. I called my family to make sure they were okay, and they were. I asked the Secret Service if they could bring my family to the White House, and the said they were bringing all the families of the chefs, who had to stay and cook.

Our families were put in the gymnasium, and they had cots in there, and we cooked for them and made sure they had plenty to eat. It made me feel really good to see all those families who were so apprehensive about their dads and moms working in the White House, and everyone was safe. There were no planes coming at us because there were no planes flying in the air and in fact, it was thirty days before the planes flew again.

I was kept in the White House for twelve days, and then the order came from President Bush that I would be flying to New York City. We flew in to New York City in helicopters, and it was weird to look into the sky and not see a single commercial plane flying anywhere.

I was sent to cook for the Fireman, Police, and EMS that the U.S. Government was providing food for. I was sent to City Hall and cooked out of the kitchen there. After we cooked the food, it was moved to Grand Central Station, and serving lines were set up for the service people come and get food.

The White House Chefs that took the trip were making certain foods. I cooked jambalaya with chicken and sausage without shrimp like no one's business, and every man and woman that ate it loved it. Many of them had never eaten that good Louisiana food before. President Bush wanted me to cook Louisiana food for those guys working so hard day after day in those horrible circumstances.

Other cooks were making hot dogs, chili, and more simple foods that were very good to taste. We made breakfasts of oatmeal, crème of wheat, and boiled eggs. We also cooked for the dogs. They were as important as people. Many folks may not know that the dogs would cut up their feet running around on the broken glass, so they had booties made for them to protect their paws. I always had a soft spot and a tear when those dogs came for food.

CHAPTER SIX
Camp David and Air Force One

I got the call to go to Camp David with President Bush. Until that time, I had not been to the Camp or flown on Air Force One. I anticipated the trip for days because it was an anomaly for me as I began to realize how far up the ladder I had come, and the experience was surreal.

We flew in a helicopter over to the camp, and the food went ahead of us in trucks, which were black unmarked vans with very dark windows. I was amazed at how beautiful and serene the place was. There is plenty to do to keep from getting bored although we were there to work. Walking trails are everywhere, and the very pretty lake is there for fishing and swimming.

When I walked into the kitchen, I couldn't believe it. Everything in there was brand new and in fact, the entire house was refurnished with new drapes, rugs, and linens because the President changes all the décor. It is a lovely place to get away for the families to relax.

The bedroom where the cooks stayed has three beds because only three chefs go to the camp at a time. You aren't allowed to roam through the house and are mainly confined to the room except when doing duties in the kitchen. I did not go every time the President went there and I would only go when he requested certain chefs make the trip. A lot of the choices had to do with the menu they were using, and the chefs who had certain skills making that type of food were invited.

We normally cooked and served for three days and then

back to the White House. I did enjoy getting to go anywhere with the President and especially to Camp David.

I waited many years before I was finally invited to fly with the President on Air Force One and make the food. The first time I walked up the rear stairs to the back of the plane and looked down that long corridor, it took my breath away. Although I am not permitted to describe every detail, I can tell everyone the plane is luxurious. Presidents are pampered, and Air Force One is one of the most fascinating in the world.

In the rear quarter, there are rows of seats with tables. Most of the food is served and eaten back there. The President has his own room of course, and sometimes I would get to go up there and take food to him. The food is not in the back of the plane where it's eaten but in the front where a galley is. The food was actually cooked in the kitchen at the white house, and then transported to the galley of the plane. The chefs heated up the food in microwaves in the galley.

The President was flying a secret mission, so no one knew he was going, and we didn't know where we were going. We couldn't tell our families, and my wife didn't know I was going to be gone. This was Thanksgiving, and it happened that we were in Afghanistan, and the President was visiting troops for the holiday. My son had not been transferred yet, so I got to see him while on this mission.

When I got back from visiting my son, I asked the President if I could talk with him privately, and he told me of course I could. This was my first trip on Air Force One, and I intended for it to be my last.

"Mr. President," I said, "I am quitting as soon as we get back to the White House."

"Why?" He asked.

"Because I am so angry at you that I can't work for you any-more."

"Why, what did I do?"

"You sent my son to war to be killed. He's been shot up twice, and you refuse to have him transferred."

"I am the President, but I can't make those kinds of decisions for the military." He explained.

"Bull shit!" I yelled. "You can do anything you want. Why don't you send your daughters to war? I bet you wouldn't."

The President ended up taking my son off the front line and sent him to Germany. He healed there, and I was expecting him to be permanently out of harm's way, but he wasn't. The Army sent him back to Afghanistan, and that's when he got shot again. A bullet was fired at the belly of the helicopter he was flying in, and the bullet ripped through his arm and leg. It was at that point I confronted the President in his office that day.

My son eventually spent twenty years with the 82nd Airborne and was honorably discharged on my birthday that year. He called me one day and told me that they were having a baby and were excited to see me. I told him that Ann is pregnant, and so the surprise was turned around. My youngest son is four weeks younger than my granddaughter.

I didn't quit my job because of Laura Bush. She put the ideas in me that the President's job becomes much more difficult during war, and that the attack on the World Trade Center had caused her husband and inordinate amount of anxiety and stress. She said he is a good man and wouldn't purposely harm anyone, and that he grieved over the boys and girls in the war, and that included my son.

I began to see that President Bush was a good husband and father, and that he cared about his country and the people he served. The lifting of my son from the battles after being twice wounded helped calm the anger deep in my soul. I won't say I ever completely forgave the President, and I wasn't completely or ever happy during his eight years as President.

CHAPTER SEVEN
President George W. Bush's Favorite Meals
How He Liked to Dress

Breakfast

The President wanted an omelet with lumped crab meat, diced Canadian bacon, shredded cheddar cheese, sliced Portobello mushrooms, green onions, and finely diced scallions. He liked dark, crispy hash browns, and orange juice with no pulp, black coffee with one sugar, cranberry juice, 1 slice of wheat bread cut diagonally.

Lunch

Texas white chili, a white smoked chicken breast, Navy beans made with white roux chicken broth, white wine, unsalted butter, olive oil, white pepper, diced jalapeno peppers, garnish on top with pepper jack cheese. The soup was served with stone ground crackers, a bowl of strawberries, and 1 bottle of Miller Lite beer.

Fast Foods

"Get me some Taco Bell," you would hear President Bush instruct his Secret Service. "Make that 1 enchilada, 2 soft tacos, some extra hot sauce, some churros, and a large lemonade."

Favorite Alcoholic Beverage

Long Neck beer and Kentucky Bourbon

How He Dressed

He loved western clothes because he's from Texas. You would spot the President in western cut Wrangler jeans, cowboy boots, western shirts with pearl buttons, a beautifully decorated belt with a big buckle. He dressed like the cowboy that he was. He also wore casual slacks and golf shirts.

★ ★ ★ ★ ★

BUSH, JR.

— Menu —

•

YELLOW & BLUE CORN, BLACK BEANS
*diced red and yellow bell peppers with a
house-made vinaigrette*

SPANISH RICE PEEL OFF
*with sautéed shrimp and crab,
sided by roasted Brussel sprouts and bacon bits*

VANILLA ICE CREAM SUNDAE
with hot fudge and roasted pecans

———— • ————

PREPARATION FOR SIX PEOPLE

SALAD

6 leaves iceberg lettuce
2 ears blue corn
2 ears yellow corn
1 16 oz can black beans
6 sprigs cilantro
1 red pepper (diced)
1 yellow pepper (diced)
1 jalapeno pepper
¼ cup fresh lime juice
1 tsp lime zest
½ cup olive oil
¼ cup apple cider vinegar
Salt to taste
Red pepper to taste

DIRECTIONS

1) Boil corn 7 min., remove and pat dry, cut kernels off cob, combine with beans in bowl.

2) Chop cilantro, dice jalapeno peppers add to bowl with olive oil, lime juice and zest, apple cider vinegar, salt and pepper, add to bowl and stir together.

3) Cover with Saran Wrap and let sit in fridge 30 min.

4) Place lettuce leaf on bottom of plate, cover with bowl mix.

5) Serve.

ENTRÉE
40 shrimp (deveined)
1 lb lump crab meat
2 tbsp crab oil
6 cups rice

1 cup clam juice
1 can Campbell's Cream of Shrimp soup
½ cup green and white onions (chopped)
4 cloves garlic (sliced)
Salt to taste
Red pepper to taste
40 Brussels sprouts
1 lb Applewood bacon

DIRECTIONS

1) Cook rice in crab oil and water.

2) Sautee shrimp in skillet until pink, add crab meat, clam juice, cream of shrimp, chopped onions, garlic, salt and pepper to taste.

3) When rice comes to temperature, fold in shrimp and crab meat, garnish with parsley.

4) Cull Brussel sprouts, cut 'x' on bottom of stems, place in salt water and olive oil for 15 min., remove, dry, cut Brussel sprouts in half, place on sheet pan, roast in oven for 10 min. at 350 degrees in oven.

5) Place bacon on sheet pan and roast in oven on separate rack with Brussel sprouts. Remove both and let cool when bacon is crispy.

6) Crumble bacon and add in bowl with Brussel sprouts, drizzle leftover bacon oil over mix.

7) Place on plate and serve.

DESSERT

Vanilla ice cream
2 cups heavy whipping cream
2 cups semi-sweet chocolate chips
Whipped cream
6 maraschino cherries

DIRECTIONS

1) Mix and melt heavy whipping cream and chocolate chips in pot over medium heat, cook until saucy.

2) Drizzle cool sauce over ice cream (3 scoops per bowl).

3) Top with whipped cream, chopped pecans or walnuts, and cherry.

4) Serve.

SECTION 5
PRESIDENT BARACK OBAMA

CHAPTER ONE
The Obamas Chose Me

I have now been in the White House for twenty-seven years or twenty years longer than I ever expected to stay. George W. Bush is gone, I am still in the house, and we have the first African American President in history. Mr. Hussein Obama is now the President, and I am the only African American White House Chef in existence. What are my chances?

The truth is I had the same insecure feelings I had been through four other times with the changing of the guard. I had been there longer than any chef in White House history. I had seen them come and go by the score. I saw Executive Chefs in Kitchen 1 get fired for all kinds of reasons. I had seen it all, and now I had to face this test one more time.

It ended up that color had nothing to do with anything. All my chefs were Caucasian, and I couldn't get an African American chef a job in my kitchen. There were two reasons for this: 1) they couldn't pass the drug test, and 2) they didn't have the credit report score needed to get hired. My entire staff in Kitchen 2 of twenty-two chefs was all white folks.

I was also the oldest chef in the kitchen, and I became a father figure to many of them, and they did not see me as an African American. They saw me as a man of morals and values and respected me.

It was all buzzing around the White House about who was going to be the next President. We were convinced that Hillary Clinton would be the next President, and we were watching

John McCain. We knew him because of the state dinners, and we would see him from time to time and talk to him. He was a good man, a Vietnam War POW and veteran. We respected him, so we weren't thinking that Barack Obama could possibly be the next president, but here he comes. He won the election easily, and history was made.

This was surreal. The first African American Master Chef in charge of a White House Kitchen would be serving the first African American President of the United States. It was black on black.

Previously, I had become a Master Chef when a letter came down to the kitchen that an opportunity was coming for the chefs working in the kitchens to go to Paris and take the test for Master Chef. No one wanted to do it because it cost fifty thousand dollars, and you would be gone for a month. There weren't enough people there who wanted to step up and take the chance of failing. I signed up for it and went to Paris.

I took the test and made the only one hundred percent ever scored up to that time. I was asked to stay and work as an instructor in Paris, and I told them I could not for two reasons. I loved my job at the White House, and I didn't want a divorce.

When I came back to the United States, I went down to New Orleans and helped open a couple of hotels that were owned by friends of President Bush, Jr. President Bush asked if I would go down there and help open a Hilton Garden Inn and Fairmont Hotel and train the staff. I did that for him, and then went back to the White House.

To fast forward, we are now looking at a new Democratic president, and they had a Republican for eight years. It was hot and heavy all over the place. We all thought the Republicans would roll on in, but it was not to be. President Bush had taken some huge hits from our involvement in the war, and the economy was sinking. It turns out the Republicans had a very weak candidate, and President Bush, Jr. was blamed for a sinking ship.

Vice President Dick Cheney had nothing but disdain for Barack Obama, and it was a daily tirade for the S.O.B. to fire all

the shots he could concerning his dislike of the African American candidate in the Democratic Party. When Barack Obama
won the election, he came to the White House with his wife and
two daughters. The Obama's were supposed to stay in the Blair
House where Vice President Cheney lived, so he made it impossible for them to stay there by filling the house to capacity with
other guests.

Because of the Vice President's choices, the Obama's had
to move into the Four Seasons Hotel. I knew something was so
wrong that things would be very uncomfortable for everybody
when Mr. Obama did come to the White House. He would come
there to visit as the newly elected president but not sworn in yet.

The President elect came to the White House with his family
and mother-in-law and started milling around meeting people
and taking in the history of the place. The Obama's toured the
White House going into every corner of it and inspecting where
they were going to live for the next four years and maybe beyond
that.

Mrs. Obama came into the kitchen, and we stood at attention. I welcomed her on behalf of our kitchen staff. She smiled
briefly but obviously had something on her mind.

"Get this stuff out of this kitchen. All of it. Get the kitchens
clean." These were Mrs. Obama's major comments after she had
seen it all. "I don't want a dish, a fork, a knife, a pot or pan, or
anything left in here. I want all the furniture removed, and every
wall freshly painted."

Staffs all around were looking at each other because they
hadn't seen this before, but I was very familiar with what happens when a new administration takes over although this was
overkill compared to the other First Ladies including Hillary
Clinton. Mrs. Obama wasn't being mean; she only wanted a fresh
start. I explained this to all of them who hadn't faced this situation and were immediately judgmental.

As chefs, we had to start cleaning everything in the kitchens
and getting invoices ready to donate the stuff that could be given
away to the shelters around the area. As we cleaned hundreds of

items, we wrapped every one of them in saran wrap. We freshly cleaned every shelf and worked over all the stoves. All the utensils used previously were taken out and given away.

Mrs. Laura Bush and Mrs. Obama got together, and Mrs. Bush took her to the warehouse. In this warehouse are antiques, furniture, and things of historic value used by Presidents down through history like no one would believe.

I was privileged to go there, and I am testifying that my impression of it was like a scene out of the movie, *Indiana Jones.* I almost wondered if the "Ark of the Covenant" could actually be in there. The items stored through history go all the way back to the George Washington era, and you can choose from them anything you like and decorate the White House any way you want.

Mrs. Obama went through the house and picked out her colors. She loves burgundy and gold, so much of the house had those color schemes. They have an elegant room where they spend time together just to talk and fellowship. The room is so beautifully decorated; it will take your breath away.

Mrs. Obama's personal color is royal blue, and she also loves turquoise. President Obama's power tie is light blue.

CHAPTER TWO
The Transition

There are always many, many meetings between the President that is leaving office, and the President who is coming into office. During one of these meetings, it was overheard that Vice President Cheney was not going to shake Mr. Obama's hand.

The day of the transition came, and President Bush was put off with Vice President Cheney because the Vice President didn't get something he badly wanted. Mr. Cheney wanted Lewis Libby pardoned after being convicted of lying to Federal officials concerning a CIA agent. It was vintage Dick Cheney to sulk and retaliate, so he and President Bush ended up not being very close friends; not that they ever were. Vice President Cheney showed up at the inauguration in a wheel chair claiming that lifting boxes during his move from the Blair House had put his back out of place. Many believed he did it so that his threat of not shaking Mr. Obama's hand would become a reality.

Barack Obama was now coming, and the transition for us had already ended. We were ready. There would be two days for the Bush's to get out of the White House. The Obama's would stay in the Blair House during that time, and President George and Laura Bush would remain right up to inauguration day.

President and Mrs. Bush came down to the kitchens to say goodbye to the entire culinary staff. They came to the kitchens one at a time instead of assembling the entire kitchen staff somewhere where they could say goodbye only once.

This is always an emotional time for many of us because we

have been cooking in some capacity for eight years, and many of us knew the President and Mrs. Bush personally. We had many one-on-one moments with them over a variety of issues from food to invitations to special events. In my case, I developed that relationship back in the George H. Bush days when President George, Jr. would visit his mom and dad. I also had expressed my deepest feelings on many occasions and my problems with his Presidency.

I was still in Kitchen 2 at this time, and I was to say goodbye to my boss the Vice President of the United States. I had already said goodbye to all the Cabinet members. Vice President Cheney would be visiting Kitchen 2, so I told my crew to back up twenty feet behind me, and I was going to say goodbye to Mr. Cheney one on one.

I now have twenty-seven people behind me. The Secret Service told me that former Vice President Cheney wouldn't have the harness on him that carried his tape recorder. He recorded every conversation he had while Vice President. Mr. Cheney now had no power or authority to do anything.

I met Mr. Cheney face to face, and this is exactly what I said when I bent down to his level in the wheel chair where he could see into my eyes and hear me clearly.

"Mr. Vice President," I began. "It has been a pleasure working for you, and I want to thank you for these eight years. You have been a very interesting Vice President, but you know what? You're a no good son-of-a-bitch."

Mr. Cheney's face turned red, but he didn't jump up and retaliate, which is what I wanted to happen. I knew he was lying about his injury, so that he wouldn't have to acknowledge that a man of another color had finally become President of the United States of America. He instructed the Secret Service to get him out of there, and they rolled him to the limousine that would take him to the inauguration.

Mr. Cheney sat away from President Bush in a wheel chair. When the oath was administered, and the United States had a new President, President Obama shook hands with former President Bush, and Dick Cheney rolled away mission accomplished. Anyone can watch the replay of that moment on television. Maybe no one really knows what happened there, but I do, and so do those people who heard Mr. Cheney show a display of anger when he said he would never shake Mr. Barack Obama's hand.

Dick Cheney was last seen being whisked away in the limousine. He did not stay for the lunch that happens after the new President is sworn into office. Mr. Cheney came back to the White House and visited his office to get the last things from his desk, and then came through the corridor where all the kitchen staff was waiting. We saluted Mr. Cheney, but I did it with my middle finger. I was never a defiant person, and this was totally out of my character. Today, I might regret that a little bit, but it shows the frustration and anger I had toward Vice President Dick Cheney.

When the President leaves the White House for the final time, he is taken away by helicopter. The Vice President goes by limousine to the airport. When they get to the airplane, the President and First Lady go up the front steps of the plane, and the Vice President walks up the rear steps.

The plane flies over the White House and then circles and flies over the White House again. As it makes its final fly over, the pilot dips the wings on the left side to say goodbye. My crew watched as the plane flew over the final time and saluted Mr. Cheney with the middle finger. These are Caucasian men who had no respect for Vice President Dick Cheney.

The Chief of Staff, Rahm Emmanuel, had the daunting task of getting the White House ready for the Obama's in two days. The whole White House was messed up, and the parade had begun up by the Capitol Building. It was like the United States had never had a president. Everything associated with President Bush was taken out of the White House. President Bush's painting had not been completed, or that would have been the only thing that remained.

The entire White House was empty including nameplates and any association with the former president. They crated the stuff and sat it on the White House lawn and in the driveways. Hundreds of painters were there with air guns and all the equipment it would take to accomplish a complete makeover in a matter of hours. New furniture was brought in, and the kitchens were completely refurbished. There was nothing left in the pantries or refrigerators. All the food would be replaced, and not one stick of butter was left in the kitchens.

The Obama's had arrived, and the White House was miraculously transformed into the home that the Obama's would call their own for the next four years. I always wondered if the Presidents moving in for the first term ever stressed over the thoughts of a second term. I am sure the first thought the Obama's had when they stood in the presence of the great historic leaders that preceded them was it would be difficult to leave the place.

We were in the kitchens when the call came for us to report to the auditorium. The Chief of Staff announced to us after we were all in there and settled,

"Ladies and gentlemen, we will be making some changes today."

I thought we had all lost our jobs, and I knew full well after being there for so many years that could happen. A female chef managed Kitchen 1, I was in Kitchen 2, and Kitchen 3 was a managed by a male chef. I was the oldest of the three chefs, and the only Master Chef that managed the kitchens.

We were standing and in walked the President with Mrs. Obama with his two daughters Malia and Sasha. Accompanying them was their mother-in-law, Mrs. Robinson.

Rahm Emmanuel, Chief of Staff, came and introduced each one. The President and Mrs. Obama were smiling from ear to ear as were the girls, being excited about becoming the First Family of the United States of America. Mrs. Robinson didn't crack a smile. She was stern, and we didn't quite know how to take her.

An announcement was made again by the Chief of Staff that there were going to be serious changes, some would be leaving, and some would be staying. The wind went out of my sails because I was excited after being through hell for the eight years with President Bush, and now the first African American President would be working with the only African American Master Chef in the White House. That was exciting to me.

You fight color everywhere. My daddy taught me that the white people who call us "colored" are missing the boat. When I was born, I was brown. When I was a child, I was brown. When I get sick, I am brown. When I lay in the sun, I stay brown, and I will die brown.

White people are born red. When they lay in the sun, they are brown. When they get sick, they are green. When they die, they turn blue. So who is colored? I used that illustration every time I had sensed one of the white people in the kitchen didn't recognized we had no color. Well, I was looking forward to being an African American chef cooking for an African American President.

CHAPTER THREE
The Official Assignment

The next meeting we had as a kitchen staff with the Obama's was a few days after things had settled down. I had seen a transition four times in my career, but I never got used to the disarray all around me. It was a pleasant relief when everything was cleaned up. I am a stickler for order, and I ran my kitchen that way, but to have the White House so messed up was more than I could stand.

The statement we were dreading finally came. The Chief of Staff made the announcement:

"Some of you here are going to stay, some of you are going to be moved around, and some of you are going to go home."

I was thinking that all my hopes of hanging on to a job this long had finally met its end, and I would be looking for another job. I thought I had that shot as an inside African American chef that would be serving the first African American president. *So that ain't gonna happen,* I thought.

"Kitchen 3 is basically going to remain the same, but some of the chefs there are going back to school," the Chief said. "In Kitchen 2, we're about to make a major change."

When this announcement was made, all I could think about was the major change was going to be me, so I braced myself for the next phase of this announcement.

"The duties of Kitchen 2 are going to be expanded to incorporate the Pentagon and specifically limited to the generals and admirals." The Chief of Staff said. "This means that you will most likely be bringing food over there. Kitchen 1 – we're going to leave you alone, but we're going to make a change for the dinner meal of the President and family."

Kitchen 1 is in charge of the president's meals, and I had never before seen a decision like this that sounded like they were going to take the dinner meal of the president out of Kitchen 1.

"The change we are going to make is to incorporate a chef from Kitchen 2 that will perform these duties."

At this point every chef listening to this announcement was looking at each other. Kitchen 2 will prepare the meal, and specifically one chef chosen from the kitchen.

"We have decided that for the longevity and professionalism of this master chef and for his dedication to all the previous presidents he has served . . ."

I am thinking, *He said, "he," and there are only two supervisors in our kitchen that are he's.* The other "he" had only been there for two Presidents, and this was my fifth one to serve.

When the Chief mentioned "Master Chef," my Sous Chef hit me in the back. "Master Chef, he's talking about you!" He exclaimed. "You're the only Master Chef here!"

Rahm Emanuel walked over to me and stuck out his hand. "I want to congratulate you for becoming President Obama's personal dinner chef."

He turned to the crowd. "Everybody, let's give a big round of applause for Master Chef Sir Ronnie Seaton!"

I was in shock, and the reality of what happened had not sunk in. "What happened?" I exclaimed.

"Ronnie, you got the gig!" My Sous Chef excitedly shouted. "You're working for the man!"

I must have been a black man who turned into a white man. That's how faint I felt. Suddenly, I looked up, and the President of the United States had walked over to me. In a straight row like a receiving line behind Mr. Obama was Michelle Obama, the two daughters, and Mrs. Robinson the mother-in-law.

President Obama put his hand on my shoulder. "Sir Master Chef Ronnie Seaton, Sr." he said. "I am looking forward to your cooking."

In disbelief or maybe it is better to express unbelief, I said to him, "Mr. President, what are you telling me?"

"You are going to be cooking my dinner meals," he explained, "but you are still going to be in charge of Kitchen 2. I don't need you in Kitchen 1. I want you to cook for my Cabinet. I want them coming to work, happy."

"Mr. President," I cried. "I may not be able to handle this assignment."

"Yes you can," he said quietly, and then raised his voice a little louder, so everyone could hear. "YES, YOU CAN!"

Mrs. Obama then stepped over. "Sir Master Chef, we need to sit down and discuss our diets, our restrictions, and how I want our food prepared."

This sounded like a direct order to me, so I never flinched. "Yes ma'am," I replied. In fact, the only thing I said to her was "Yes ma'am."

"I will be in touch with you tomorrow," she said.

"Yes ma'am," I replied.

Malia Ann and Sasha wanted to say something to me. "Master Chef – can we come down to the kitchen and work with you?"

"Of course you can, ladies," I replied.

"Can we bake cookies and make pizzas?"

"You can make all the cookies and pizzas you want to make," I said.

The stern faced no nonsense Mrs. Robinson never said a word to me, but I said to her, "Mrs. Robinson, I will be in touch with you and let you know what we're planning on cooking for the weekends. You and I will work close together."

Mrs. Robinson said to me without a smile or nod, "You will see me prior to the Saturday and Sunday dinners, and I will help you with the preparation. Do you understand?"

"Yes ma'am," I said.

By this time, everyone in the room was staring at me. "You gotta new king now, Master Chef," my Sous Chef said with a big smile on his face. Everybody was happy for me.

Two days later, Mrs. Obama met with me, and we meticulously went over the menu noting every detail as to what food her husband liked, and what she liked. I then met with the girls, and they informed me what kind of cookies they wanted to make, and other treats they were interested in leaning how to bake.

I then met with the toughest one of them all – Mrs. Robinson. The mother-in-law was a game changer. She came at me with a list of ingredients and instructions on prepping the food for the meals on Saturdays and Sundays. I never saw it coming.

"Master Chef, you will prep all these meals when I tell you which ones we're having on the weekends. You will cook nothing. I will do all the cooking on Saturdays and Sundays. Do you understand and can you adhere to this?"

Man, I was beside myself. I couldn't believe this massive diversion of the White House presidential protocol for weekend meals. I looked into Mrs. Robinson's eyes and knew I better drop anything that I might argue and obey the rules.

"By the way," she said. "You will prep the food on Fridays and bring it to the apartment by the residence."

I prepared my kitchen staff to run the gauntlet. The President would eat at the hotel for the first week while we got all the food ready and restocked the entire kitchen, which up to this time had been completely emptied, and the food given to the shelters.

The first meal we made for the Obama family was to become famous.

Salad - baby spinach with the stems removed. We mixed in feta cheese with toasted pine nuts, strawberries, blackberries, and blueberries. We dropped in English walnuts from California. The dressing was raspberry vinaigrette.

Soup - French onion made with Kobe beef tips. Kobe beef originated in Japan and has a high fat content that makes it soft and tasty. Red onions were cooked with Brandy, beef broth, olive oil, a little butter, Berlize Creole bread on top, and melted mozzarella cheese.

Tangerine Sorbet - I had never made a tangerine sorbet, but I made this one.

Main Course - Meat Loaf mixed with beef and pork, and our homemade bread crumbs. Oregano thyme and sage was added, salt and pepper, Worchester sauce, egg, a little heavy cream. We made these ingredients into the meat loaf but in the middle, we added boiled eggs. They were placed in such a way that when the meat loaf was sliced, you could see the white and yellow circles. The meatloaf was wrapped in thick bacon and glazed with an orange marmalade.

The starch was duchess potatoes from the aforementioned Jacqueline Kennedy era, which are Yukon Gold potatoes with heavy cream. President Obama had heard about these potatoes, so he added some salt and pepper nutmeg, a little wine, and French butter. You put these mixed ingredients through a ricer, put them into a pastry bag, piped out, brushed with an egg wash, and re-baked again. The second time you bake these potatoes; they will come out looking like a rose.

President Obama loves asparagus. We made white and green asparagus with a béarnaise sauce. This is a sauce made with tarragon, fresh cream, white wine, salt and pepper nutmeg, and a little rosemary.

Dessert - Chocolate cake with a Ganache icing and chocolate covered strawberries on top.

This was the first meal I served to President Obama, and it became his favorite that was made for him many times during the seven years I spent with the family.

President Obama has a very diverse pallet. He loves African, Chinese, Italian, Japanese, Korean, Mexican, and all kinds of American cuisine. It was never difficult when it came to satisfying his tastes. Interestingly, he only ate fried foods two times a year. These days were the Fourth of July and Labor Day. In fact, these were the only two days of the year that fried food was served anywhere in the White House.

President Obama never made my kitchen staffs work late at night or ever imposed on us like other presidents often would. He understood we had families, and he came into the kitchen and told us that whatever our religious beliefs were, we were to honor that day on it's day of worship.

We always had the opportunity to go to church, and it was never denied. Our schedules reflected around our religious beliefs. I have to make this statement. This was not the rule with the other Ppresidents whether written or unwritten. Work came first with the other presidents although they all understood family needs as President Obama did.

President Obama understood that prior to his coming on board, we had endured many hardships. The economy affects us just like it does everyone else. We had gone through eight years of a tumultuous presidency, and we were battered. He wanted to help repair that in us, so I believe he lessened the load whenever he could to accommodate our family and personal needs.

First Lady Michelle Obama took a direct interest in everything going on in the kitchens. She wanted healthy eating. She changed the menus more than once to ensure that anyone eating anywhere in the White House was eating healthy food. She changed to organic food and aquaponics. The White House has it's own aquaponic gardens where everything is freshly grown in the greenhouses.

I was fascinated when we first brought these gardens into the White House and received special training on how the gardens grow vegetables in water. I also loved to watch the Koi fish swim in the water. Their droppings fertilize the growth of the vegetables and they keep the tanks completely clean.

Mrs. Obama had the people from Disney World come and install the science of aquaponics in the White House because they've been experts at the science since 1982 at Disney World.

President Obama told us that the White House wasn't the White House; it is the people house. He said, "People have a right to come to the White House and take a tour. It is their house. They have a right to see where the leader of the country lives and performs the duties as President of the United States of America."

The first time I ever heard a President tell his staff, or at least the kitchen staff, that the people of America don't work for him; he works for them. This first African American President of the United States impacted us as did his wife.

When I was selected as the Dinner Chef, Mrs. Obama yelled to the Secret Service, "bring it in."

They rolled in a cart with a CD player on it. She then told us to raise our right hands. We thought we were going to take an oath of some kind. She then told us to bend our hand over our heads.

President Obama, Chief of Staff Emanuel, the Secret Service, and the girls were doing it. She told us that when the song comes on, she wants us to repeat the words of the singer.

"Say it loud, I'm black, and I'm proud." It was James Brown.

The only black people in the room were the Obama's and I, so we were into it. She stopped the tape and then lectured the crowd.

"Ladies and gentlemen, you don't understand. We're all going to do this. Okay?" She instructed us in a very serious no nonsense tone. She meant for everybody to get involved even if they did think it was silly, and there was no doubt many of them were uncomfortable.

"Now, I am going to turn this music back on, and you are going to wave your hands over your heads and sing, "There's a new sheriff in town; he's black, and he's proud."

Mrs. Obama turned the tape on, and we all sang the tune while waving our hands over our heads. It was surreal to witness how she made all these people obey her. She suddenly turned off the tape. All was silent.

"You people," she exclaimed. "This is a joke!"

That did it. Everybody laughed and laughed, and we had more fun welcoming this vibrant First Lady than we'd ever had before. She told us that her husband worked for her when they got out of law school, and that's how they met.

"Behind every man is a great woman," Michelle Obama said, "and behind every woman is a great man. We're here as a team, and this is the People House."

Everybody was asking me if we have to sing that song everyday, and I told him or her, "you might want to learn the song."

Mrs. Obama is a great lady, and is a wonderful First Lady.

She did not have the sweetness of Barbara or Laura Bush, and she was not the ransacking angry woman that Hillary Clinton was, but she did have one thing in common with Mrs. Clinton. Authority. She not only wanted to be in charge, she took charge. She never hurled and broke expensive objects that I witnessed, and she never cursed.

Mrs. Obama never raised her voice, but she has an air about her that makes you notice that she is a stickler for detail and accountability. One of the things I respected about her the most was the fact you could walk into her office and talk to her. She may disagree with you and would make no hesitation letting you know that, but she never betrayed your confidences. What happened in her office, stayed in her office. She hated gossip and rumors. She always said the most destructive things against making something work were rumors that contained a pack of lies.

I have never seen Mrs. Obama hit her husband or disrespect him in any way. She makes no bones about the fact that she loves her husband and family. She is task oriented and punctual like Mrs. Clinton, but she is not aggressive like Mrs. Clinton was.

Michelle Obama insists that the family prays every night. The rumor is that when the President is out of town, he has to get on the speakerphone and pray with his family. Mrs. Obama insists that the President is accessible to her no matter where in the world he may be.

I want to go on record by saying that all the presidents cheated on their wives except President Obama. The practice of extra marital affairs has a very long history among the Presidents of the United States. President Obama is a family man and if he weren't, his mother-in-law, Mrs. Robinson, would make sure he walked the line.

It was rumored in the kitchen one afternoon that someone heard Mrs. Obama tell her husband,

"Be careful who you kiss on because you know where you lay your head."

Mrs. Obama checks out the president's clothes. She smells his shirts, checks his underwear, and makes him accountable.

There was a time when President Obama kissed a lady in a crowd and when he got home, there were some heavy words about it. Mrs. Obama and his mother-in-law jumped him.

Michelle Obama is more intelligent than the President. He worked for her when he was an up and coming lawyer. He does write his own speeches, and I believe Mrs. Obama approves them. They aren't lawyers for no reason.

Mrs. Obama has a strong affinity for New Orleans. She loves the people there because she says they are the friendliest in America. She was always sorry to see New Orleans people leave the White House, but a lot of people just can't take the pressure seven days a week. You can't have skeletons in the closet because your life is transparent, and it will all come to light sooner or later.

The First Lady has me involved with her program to kick obesity that plagues our children. New Orleans is the number one city in America for obese children. Michelle Obama's "Kick Obesity" program involves Grand Master Eric O'Neal, and I help him in this campaign called "The One Million Kick Challenge" that teaches kids to kick obesity through defense, education, and fitness.

Mrs. Obama works for the families of the veterans as well as all families in America. She wants to make sure they get post-traumatic stress treatment, job training, and that their families are cared for properly. She is a leader and proponent of family values.

Mrs. Obama doesn't hide anything from the public. She is definitely transparent and loves her family. It was always nice to take food up to the residence. By the way, the Obama residence at the White House is breathtaking. I used to carry food I'd prepared up there, and it was heart warming to see the President holding one of his girls and asking her how her day had been. He would lift one up and put her on his shoulders. The public does not know all this about the President and Mrs. Obama because Mrs. Obama keeps the family life private.

Monday, Tuesday, and Wednesdays are family nights for the

Obama's. Thursday nights, the President will dance a nice romantic slow dance before they sit down to eat. He will dip her, and she will say "Oh, Barack!" The girls will giggle, and Mrs. Robinson smiles because this exercise shows all the signs of a loving family unit.

Before every meal, the Obama's pray and ask God's blessing on the family and the country. They thank the Lord for the food. They get into a circle to pray. Each one has a certain night they lead the prayer and on Wednesdays, they invite me into the circle, and I lead in prayer. I prayed just like they did. I prayed for the country, and for the world, and for the President of the United States and his family.

I should also include in my story something more about the first kids. My favorite children were the Obama girls. Chelsea Clinton was my next favorite, and President George and Laura Bush had the worst behaved children while I was in my career at the White House.

The Obama children were friends with my kids, and they all spent time in the kitchen learning to cook when my children came over there. My sons, Xavier and Samir, were close in age to Sasha and Malia. They ran around together whenever the boys would come over to the White House to visit.

I do know that Chelsea spent some time learning to cook from the Chef over in Kitchen 1 when President Bill Clinton was in office. The other children in the White House took no interest in learning to cook. They only came by to request something.

CHAPTER FOUR
Reflections from Kitchen One

I was moved to Kitchen 1. I was not the head of the kitchen, but I was equal in authority to the Head Chef of the Kitchen. I had worked from the ground up over thirty plus years. I moved from Kitchen 3 to Kitchen 2, and now I am in Kitchen 1.

My promotion made a big stir among all the White House kitchens. They were all talking about it. I decided that the only way for me to keep from having enemies was to go talk to everyone, and so I did. I went from kitchen to kitchen and talked to the staff in each one. I told them that I was their friend, and I knew what it was to work from a low position, so I would help them. I was experienced, so there was nothing they were going to experience on a daily basis that I had not seen, heard, or done before including a terrorist bombing, God forbid.

I made friends with everybody, and so the operations became much smoother as everyone became cooperative, and we lived Mrs. Obama's dream, and that was to be a team. She preached that constantly, and I was going to carry her wishes down the line. I did more than just cook, and the job in Kitchen 1 helped me meet a lot of the needs the cooks had.

President Obama was famous for showing up somewhere in the White House and slipping out under the noses of the Secret Service. We had all seen him walking and observing, and taking in everything he could. There wasn't an inch of the White House that President Obama had not seen. I've seen the President sitting on Abraham Lincoln's bed.

One of the privileges of being the top chef in Kitchen 1 was the free rein to move about the White House. Previously, I was under the censorship of the Secret Service and not allowed in certain areas of the buildings. There were many rooms I had not seen or knew existed. Now, I could move about wherever I wanted to go. I had clearance to visit any area of the White House excluding the private residence. I had my own Secret Service agent assigned to me, and he followed me everywhere.

The movement to Kitchen 1 also affected the economics of my household. People working at the White House don't make the money that some might think. I struggled with bills and the costs of raising eight kids. In Kitchen 3, I was on a salary of $40,000.00 per year. I moved from that income to $129,000.00 per year in Kitchen 1, and it took thirty-four years to get there, so we don't come out of the White House wealthy people. With my salary, Ann and I thought we died and went to heaven. As a Master Chef being as skilled as I am, I could easily command twice or three times that amount of money working in a top class restaurant.

I did have some great perks. I didn't have to pay for anything to be dry cleaned. All my clothes were cleaned at the White House. I was not allowed to travel to and from work in my chef's uniform, so I wore Duck Head clothes with tennis shoes and a windbreaker jacket. I showered at home but took another shower when I got to work.

We got a discount on our food for the family. We had a special card that we used at a certain grocery, and the discount was substantial for the White House staffers. We were given passes to theatres, museums, and other places for the public to be entertained.

I received free haircuts anytime I wanted them. The barbers are in the White House to attend to the staff with these privileges. I wanted to look fresh every day, so I had a haircut and shave every morning at 4:00 a.m. Once a month, I would visit the dentist and have my teeth inspected and cleaned if necessary in order to keep my smile showing nice white teeth.

I was given a free gym membership and received deep dis-

counts on the airlines. We were also given bonuses that amount-
ed to fifty dollars for a performance of not missing work to a
couple hundred dollars for being on time with our meals. These
bonuses didn't happen once or twice a year; they were constant,
so we got a healthy increase in income by the bonus system. I
was very thankful for those perks.

One of the bonuses worth mentioning was for the lack of
theft. Nothing was ever stolen from my kitchen, but workers did
steal. Occasionally, some one would get caught on camera taking
stuff out of the kitchen.

Probably the most blatant case of theft while I was working
for President Obama was a guy who stole a twenty-pound block
of shrimp and was carrying it in his backpack. The cost of the
shrimp was around two hundred dollars. He stole it and then
forgot to take it out of his pack. While he was walking down the
hall on his way out, Security saw him and said that his backpack
was leaking.

When the man denied that there was anything in his bag
that could be leaking, the guard asked to inspect it. Inside was
melting frozen shrimp. The man was arrested and then called
me to ask for help. He was from Kitchen 3 and had worked for
me in that kitchen. I told him that there was no way I could help
him. He knew what he was doing, so he would have to face the
consequences. He lost his job and went to jail for six months. I
supported his family for those six months and made sure they
had everything they needed that I could provide.

During the George W. Bush administration, thefts were ram-
pant in the kitchens. Everyone thought that when President
Obama came on board that things would get even more relaxed,
but they didn't. President Obama tightened down the security
several notches making it more difficult to get away with these
kinds of crimes.

No matter how much security and everything else the Secret Service can do, thefts still take place. Some of the cooks will
hook up with the delivery trucks and move food out through
that avenue. They will then meet somewhere to transport the

food where it has been previously sold. We were all aware, but I kept a tight rein on my kitchen and never had one thing stolen that I know about.

You can't be very much in debt and work at the White House. People find out you have large credit card debts, and your back's against the wall, and they will offer to pay off your bills for favors. It happens even at the highest level in the nation.

You can't get into the White House with keys. Your eyeball is scanned, and you can't have facial hair. Beards and moustaches can be faked and cover a disguise. I saw this security tighten and tighten over the years but under President Obama, it was the tightest.

I intended to work for the Obama administration until President Obama's last term was finished. Because of my medical conditions, I had to step out and into semi-retirement. I live on disability income because I had to retire under medical, so I will get my full retirement from my work for thirty-four years when I reach the age of sixty-five. I am sixty-two years old now, but I'm in no hurry. I am starting my Culinary School, and that will allow some income. This book will definitely make my wife happy because right now, she's the breadwinner of the house. I also can make some money doing private dinners, etc.

Ann put me through school, so I will be happy to give back to her from the book project. She is now working on her Ph.D. as a first grade teacher. I am working on building an entire school with all the arts. Music, dancing, singing, and of course cooking... We intend to spend the rest of our lives in this venture to help our community that has had an awful time recovering from Hurricane Katrina. New Orleans was devastated by that disaster, and I'm not sure if we will ever recover.

We are going to add a facility where special education is part of the plan and process. ADHD, Autistic kids, blind kids, and any child needing special education help. Ann Seaton will be Principal, and I will be the Head Master. We will most likely get Government assistance to pull this off, but we are looking forward for that time to come.

I want to leave a legacy for my kids. I spent the better part of my life behind the fences of the White House, and my family never got to see me very much for all those years. I missed a lot that I want to make up.

CHAPTER FIVE
The Obama Presidency

Nobody working in the White House when President Obama came on board recognized him to be anything but a novice. We were all in consensus that he was probably the most unseasoned person to ever hold the office in the history of the United States presidency. I am not on the inside of politics even at the White House, but I wondered how an African American with so little experience could possibly get elected President of the United States. I was happy he did, but I felt some uneasiness concerning how he would fare. I had a ton of knowledge watching the other presidents for thirty years, so I knew when a man was over his head, and Mr. Obama was definitely over his head.

President Obama had more meetings at the beginning of his terms than I had ever seen from any of the other Presidents. Obviously he was stressed with the rigors of the new job, and that would be the same for every President that steps into the Oval Office for the first time. President Obama was requiring even more attention, and that was weighing on the staff. One thing he never did was raise his voice at one of the staff members or slam his fist on the table. I've seen First Ladies carry on like that.

Michelle Obama is a very nice lady. She smiles a lot and unlike many of the public that may have the opposite opinion, she is a pleasant person. The girls were never demanding, but Mrs. Obama had put them outside the White House to attend a regular school. She wanted the girls to grow up mainstream. The kitchen would get involved when the girls wanted to provide food for their class, so we would prepare the food, and the Secret Service would take it over to the school and set it up. This was always a treat, and I am sure one the students in the classroom will never forget.

There were long nights at the White House; especially, when the military was looking for Osama Bin Laden. There were some very heated conversations in the rooms I delivered food. The military didn't respect the President for knowledge in how to pursue anything militarily. I am only giving my opinion, but I do know what I observed. I felt this was grating on the President because he was the junior in the room; not the military experience in the room.

I was supervising bringing food into one of these late night meetings, and I overhead one of the staffers say to President Obama, "You're a stupid idiot. You don't know one thing about what you're doing."

I heard a lot because I was the one who prepared the President's food, and no one except me. No one approached the President with any food from anywhere but me. Within one week of being in office, President Obama was receiving serious death threats, so the Secret Service watched the situation much more closely than when things were more relaxed. We had to run to the basement three times in a week. One of these incidents was when someone had left an unsupervised bag on the sidewalk, so we hit the basement running.

President Obama was taken to a bunker during these threats. He did more running than a track star. Finally, concrete barricades were put up to keep people and cars from coming too close and dropping stuff off. President Obama was early on the way to becoming the president who would receive more death threats than all the other presidents depending on what you're reading. He at least has received as many as four times the threats that President Jimmy Carter received while in office.

The most frightening thing that happened to me since being captured in Vietnam was when I was told that there was a threat on my life. When I questioned why anyone would want to kill me, I was told, "You are working for the man, and the "N" word is dropping all over the country."

President Obama is a family man, even though, some people may think he is not. He ate dinner with his family every night. The only exception was when a working meeting was taking place that would go into the long hours of the evening. Another thing, Mrs. Robinson would call him every day at 4:00 p.m. and ask him what time he was coming home. It was hard for President Obama to tell the First Mother he wasn't coming home in time for dinner.

My entire routine changed. Over these years that I have been reporting, I had developed certain habits. After years and years of religiously doing the same things over and over, I had to get completely used to another protocol. I was promoted to a different job, so the rules changed.

I have to get used to a totally different protocol. Of course I had seen how the chefs at my level operated, but this would be my first and new experience as a Master Chef. I was now at work at 3:00 a.m. and would head to my office, unlock the door, and turn on the lights. I would then get the production sheet from the previous day, and then take a walk through the kitchen. I checked all the racks making sure everything was prepared and ready for the day. If somebody's rack wasn't ready, I would put a star on it, and that person knew when he or she showed up at 5:00 a.m., they would have to come and see me.

This was a two-hour walk through. Every thing used in the White House can be rolled away and stored. All the hoses that are electrical or gas are extended for safety, and nothing is left to chance. That was the responsibility I had with the job.

At 5:00 a.m., the crew arrives in the kitchen. At 6:00 a.m., we have a staff meeting. Breakfast had to be ready at 7:28 a.m. When breakfast is served, we start working on lunch. After lunch we begin working on dinner. After dinner is served, we start working on breakfast. This is a never-ending cycle that carries on seven days a week without interruption. Nothing is ever late, and nothing is done nonchalant.

I now worked from 3:00 a.m. to 10:00 p.m. every night except the weekends. I had weekends off unless there was something special going on that required my services, or if it was requested that I be present or do the cooking. I was there nineteen hours every day. The reason I did not work on the weekends was because I prepped for Mrs. Robinson on Fridays, and she did the cooking for the family Saturdays and Sundays.

Master Chefs wore the traditional jacket to work on most days. It was a white jacket with black trim with the White House seal on it. We would change colors of jackets depending on what we were going to do. If we wore black, it meant that it was a cleanup day.

We would wear a red jacket when somebody was going to get terminated. The person was never terminated in front of everybody. He or she would be taken to an office, and another representative would be with them. If it was a man in question, a man would be there and likewise a woman would be the representative if a female were in question. The red jacket was a natural deterrent to bad behavior. If you saw the Master Chef walk in with a red jacket, you knew something was going down.

A green jacket meant someone was going to get a pay raise, and a denim jacket meant we were going to be cooking outdoors on the White House lawn. A gold jacket meant that somebody was going to be promoted. Gray jackets were worn when we were ready to prepare and serve a State dinner. Only the supervisors wore these jackets, and all the others wore traditional white jackets and black pants. The kitchen staff wore no checkered or patterned slacks.

Supervisors wear a tall white hat while the kitchen staff wears a white skullcap with an elastic band on the back. No one is allowed to wear paper hats because they can easily fall off and into the food. Everyone wars gloves, and every two hours you change your gloves and re-sanitize. You sign your name in a book denoting that you have done this. If you do not sign your name, you were required to visit the supervisor in his office after work.

We listened to music while we were cooking food. We had

lots of music archived. We liked to prep the food to the music of Mozart. We cooked to the music of a lady named Enya, and when it was time to clean up, we each picked a song. There are five songs we picked, and we had fifteen minutes to get out of the kitchen.

When the fifth song ended, the cooks needed to be out of the kitchen, so the stewards could come in and clean the entire kitchen. The last person to leave would be around 9:30 p.m., and I would stay until 10:00 p.m. I would head home but still needed to be back in the kitchen at 3:00 a.m. If there was something special going on, I may not get to go home at all but grab a couple hours sleep and back to work. The White House provided special room for the kitchen staff when there was a need to stay over.

The rooms were equipped with everything we needed including lockers. We would turn our clothes into the laundry, and we had a couple extra sets of clothes in the lockers when we needed them.

Except on occasion, the meals for the Obama's were very simplistic, and they never went overboard with their demands about food. Mr. Obama wanted to save money. He didn't see a need for over spending just because he had an unlimited expense account. We found him extremely sensitive in that area.

The products we bought for the kitchen weren't bad or "cheap," they just weren't luxury and over the top. I like Mr. Obama's way of working with the budget. The only time things got fancy was the State dinners. President Obama didn't spare any expense in entertaining world leaders because food can change the course of negotiations or ice down a fragile plan that needed ratifying between two nations.

THE BIRTH CERTIFICATE CONTROVERSY

When President Obama's right to be president was being challenged by the pundits who didn't believe he was born in the United States, including Donald Trump, the controversy was the focus of everyday gossip in every place where people worked in the White House. You couldn't get away from it, and everybody was consumed by it.

In my kitchen, we handled the theories this way: If he had gotten far enough to become a Senator of the United States from Illinois, and then got screened every way there was by the Central Intelligence Agency of the United States and still made it, we had no problem with the legitimacy of the birth certificate. We looked at the whole matter as Republican hoopla trying to discredit him.

President Obama's mother is Irish, and his father was a natural-born African. His grandparents, who were Irish, raised President Obama. His mother remarried, so he had siblings of other races. The bottom line was that if the President said he was born in the United States, then that was good enough for us. If there were any legitimate questions, they would have been able to disprove it easily.

There are some concerns, and we all knew they should be answered. For instance, the birth certificate uses the language "African American," and we all know the African Americans back then never used that term. In fact, it was never thought of or used until the last few years. I worked over these thoughts trying to figure out why they let the birth certificate come out with that language on there but never could figure it out, so I didn't listen to the gossip and went on about my work. On my birth certificate from New Orleans that was hand written, they issued the certificate with my race classified as "Negro."

The African American culture has been identified by lots of different names. My daddy and mother were "colored," then we were negroes, Afro Americans, black, and now they use the words African American. Since I was the only African American in my kitchen, the other staff members kept their distance in talking to me too much about it because they respected me, and knew it could be a sensitive area.

VICE PRESIDENT JOSEPH BIDEN

Vice Presidents are an important part of the presidency; even though, people don't give too much credence to the job they do. Folks think it is a worthless figurehead job, but it isn't.

When you are close by everyday and live what goes on with our Presidents, you get to know the necessity of this office.

Of the five vice presidents I worked for, Mr. Biden was the one that worked mostly "out of the box." The Vice President would say some things that upset the president, but they always seemed to work it out. Mr. Biden had strong family values and integrity. He is a strong church going man and prays. How do I know these leaders practice praying? Because they would pray in front of us, including President Obama.

Vice President Biden was probably the least demanding of any of the presidential leaders. He never put heavy burdens on us like making us stay late to cook, and then forget we're there. If there was a crisis, he would have the Chief of Staff inform us what the protocol would be, and I believe it was because of his sensitivity in placing a burden on us. In other words, he treated the kitchen staff like human beings instead of slaves.

He never asked for anything exotic but seemed to be mindful that we weren't servants catering to someone's every whim. The one thing about Mr. Biden that stands out is the fact that he never once, that I heard, disrespected the President. He has a great sense of humor like President Obama has, so they complimented each other.

I don't agree with a lot of what the Vice President believes, but I like him. I still talk to him, and he always asks me how my family is before we talk about anything else. He has discussed some political issues with me just for conversation. He's interested in what people think; even though, most could never affect the outcome of a decision. He was not a proponent of same sex marriage. He was strong at that time about marriage being a union between a man and a woman.

The Vice President didn't accept abortion in any sense and voiced his opinion that every child has a right to be born. He believed that life begins at conception, so he follows the Catholic Church doctrine on the matter. He said one time that he's been a Catholic all his life and supports the Church's position that abortion is wrong in any sense.

Vice President Biden had a strong belief that people should work for a living, so he was critical of pandering and making a career out of receiving welfare. People criticize Mr. Biden because he doesn't come out strong on these issues, but he is careful about undermining the president's position although he may not agree with him. His outlook is that everybody should either have a higher education or a trade and skill.

CHAPTER SIX
The Demeanor of President Obama
Leaving My Post

President Obama came into the White House a heavy cigarette smoker. Mrs. Robinson, who wastes no energy making sure everyone knows where she stands, forced the President to quit smoking. She told him that he would smell like smoke and not like the leader of the free world should smell. He would drop ashes all over the place, and she wasn't going to put up with that. Mrs. Robinson had a patch delivered to the president and forced him to wear it. He no longer smokes.

The President swims every morning and likes to play basketball, but he isn't very good at it. He loves golf, and this has gotten him into trouble more than once while he was assuaging his addiction. He was ignoring, according to some people, his God called duty as President. I believe golf relaxes the President, and he gets a lot done talking to the guests he invites to play golf with him. I've lots of experience making food and serving during the golf games of the presidents, so I know the importance of playing golf is more than a game to them.

President Obama is a very serious person, but he will smile when you least expect it. He is very articulate and can talk as intelligently as any president I worked for with the exception of Ronald Reagan. No president could communicate like President Reagan.

President Obama did have a golden moment when he invited Nawaz Sharif, Prime Minister of Pakistan, to the White House. The buzz all over the White House was concerning how

President Obama would handle the situation because he has a Muslim name. The parties didn't know what direction he would take in meeting this man.

Security was as high for this meeting as I had seen in over thirty years. Every cooking utensil, dinnerware, and food was scrutinized like we hadn't seen it happen before. I believe this meal was the most difficult that I prepared at the White House in all the years, and that included some really tough ones.

I think the event with the Prime Minister of Pakistan was the catalyst that escalated my health to turn for the worse. I worked around the clock for two straight days without sleeping. I was weak and about to pass out when my crew told me to stop and lie down, and they would wake me in three hours. I did sleep and woke three hours later. It felt good enough for me to carry on, and I felt much better.

We had to make sure the meal was perfect. The affair was well planned and orchestrated down to the translators making sure not one word in transition was translated differently than what was being said. That was not always the situation when meetings had to have every word translated correctly.

The food for the meal was American food mixed with some of the dishes from their country. The President was very eloquent but cautious. He was more careful than most of the times you would see him operate. It seems he was clearly conscious of every word he was saying.

During the conversations, it was predetermined that when the President said a certain thing, everyone was to clap. When he made the statement, no one in the room applauded. When that happened, there was a buzz across the entire banquet hall. The President looked irritated, so he said it again, and then the applause happened. It was probably louder than it would have been if the audience hadn't missed the punch line the first time. It turned out the tension was created by a poor translation to guests. When they did not react, the crowd certainly wasn't going to clap and create tensions that had not been planned.

During all this time, I was focused on the food and stressed as to whether it would be right. Would it be warm enough? These dinners were prepared slightly undercooked. Before the meal is carted all the way up to the dining halls, the food is put in hotboxes to finish cooking, and then should be perfectly done and hot as it is placed on the tables.

We dropped two hundred plates at one time. It is something to see when this happens. Just imagine six waiters placing the food on a table at once. Now visualize the beauty of ten plates per table being put down at once. It's like watching a synchronized marching band playing at a football halftime.

This was my last official State dinner, and I was really proud to end my career on a high note like that. It is something I will never forget. I was asked if I would come back to the White House for special events if they needed me. I told them,

"All you have to do is ask. I will always come back and cook whatever you need."

President Obama is still the President for the next year and a half while this book is being written, and people have found out what we in the kitchen know about him. He's a great negotiator, and he won't take "no" for an answer.

The President never uses the words, "I can't."

"If you don't' try, how do you know?" He would tell us.

They're on him about immigration. I was talking to Mr. Obama one day about this. "Master Chef, why are they on me about all this? Don't they know that every person in America is an immigrant except the American Indian?"

We were sitting at a table with President Obama one day when he was complaining about the Republicans not being honest about Social Security.

"They would have jeopardized their own grandmothers with this kind of rhetoric," he commented.

These kinds of conversations happened when the President would ask us to sit down and talk. He was always interested in what we thought. It was funny, a president talking to some cooks about the politics of the nation.

The President also talked about the changes we make sometimes in the kitchen. Food affects a president, and people may not think about that. The President can't have gas, or diarrhea that could cause embarrassments or a meeting to cancel altogether. If he had a problem and it is determined not to be a bug of some sort, he will come down and ask if we changed the way we made that particular food.

One of the most sensitive controversies among the kitchen concerning the President's policies or social doctrine was the "alternative lifestyle" of some folks. The kitchen staff is made up of all sorts of religions and politics. They discuss the issues just like the public does, and they may voice their opinions privately among themselves. President Obama explained that he is the President of all the people, and their lifestyles shouldn't make a difference.

The President did not interfere, but he was clear to us about something the media would never report because they may not know. President Obama told us that if we are of that lifestyle, don't impose it on everybody else, and keep it to ourselves. He said for anybody who may have those tendencies to stay consistent to who they are. Don't go home James and come back Jamie. Controversial? Yes it is, but it is no different working in the kitchen behind the protected sanctity of the White House than anywhere else.

President Obama would not allow anyone to date while on duty. Single people coming into the kitchen were frowned upon if an affair began with a married man or woman, so he allowed no dating for anyone married or single. More than once, families would come to visit, and their husband, wife, dad, or mom would be standing in a compromising position and much too close to the opposite sex. That was a recipe for trouble that the President and Mrs. Obama did not want among their staff.

The President did not interfere with religious beliefs. You could be an atheist or agnostic or an evangelical charismatic. It didn't matter. Just like the lifestyle matters, you could not bring religious issues up at work. There is no place for evangelism in the White House from any sect of religion.

Politics was to be kept to us. President and Mrs. Obama talked all the time to us about these issues. They wanted a strongly connected staff; not a divided one. Mrs. Obama had a poem that she gave to us and wanted us to read it all the time to remind us that we were not to tear each other down but to lift each other up. All the moral values were private and personal. I will say there was more harmony in my kitchen under President Obama than any of the other Presidents I served. I don't say that because I am an African American; I say this because I believe it's the truth.

Being President of the United States has to be the hardest job in the world. This is the reason all of them come into the White House with a full head of colored hair and leave there with a full head of gray hair. Mr. Obama turned gray very quickly, and I know some it has to do with natural age, but most of it has to do with the stress a president is under 24/7.

The decisions of a president affect the entire world, and he has to carry that burden. Deaths occur sometimes because of the mistakes that are made through presidential orders. The President's family is under stress as well wondering if he is going to come home from a trip and survive all those death threats that are made against them.

All my opinions have been inside of me for a very long time, and I don't intend to use this book to spill them out. All the Presidents I worked for had a profound hand in shaping who I am today as did their wives. None of them affected my politics or influenced who I voted for. I voted for candidates that I didn't work for because I am neither Democrat nor Republican when working in the kitchen.

I did not support President Obama's decisions in many, many things, and we are on the opposite side of many issues. I stayed loyal to the office and respected the man in power; even though, I didn't agree with him.

I am making a commercial for a Republican running for office in Louisiana, and I am a Democrat. I was called by the White House and asked why I was supporting a Republican. My answer was that I'm not working for the White House anymore, and I am free to do what I please. Of course while working in the White House kitchens, speaking out was never a privilege afforded to me.

I am not a liberal and don't like liberal politics. I believe every man should work, or he shouldn't eat. I hate welfare, and I have eight children that I raised. I don't like Section 8, food stamps, and every couple ought to think before they bring kids into the world. Everybody is not a parent, and I feel a lot is wrong in this country because our nation doesn't understand that. Being a parent is a privilege, and child molesters and abusers should receive more punishment than what is handed to them sometimes.

I cut my tenure short with President Obama in January of 2015 after 34 years as a White House Chef. I did not leave because of any disagreements or maltreatment by the President or Mrs. Obama. I left because of medical reasons. I had a heart attack and had to have an operation to place stints. Although I recovered and could still work, there were other things going on with me. If we had to run to the basement to flee something threatening us, I would never make it. My legs are gone, and I wear braces on both legs.

I was driving my car one day, and I couldn't feel the accelerator or the brake pedal. My hands were numb, and I couldn't grip the steering wheel. I started losing the vision in my right eye, so it was time for me to leave. I would go to President Obama and speak to him about it.

I did speak to President Obama and told him that I needed to leave my post after 34 years. He did not want me to leave and in fact asked me to stay because the doctors could handle all the medical problems. One of my crew members told me:

"Master Chef, you get a check just like we do. You need to handle this your own way."

I decided to leave. I talked to the First Family and told them of my decision. I went home and talked it over with my family. We agreed that when you can't enjoy your work anymore, it is time to go. I needed to get healed in many ways, and the only way to do that was to go home.

When I arrived back at the White House, it was now my duty to find a replacement or at least recommend a replacement for me in the kitchen. I gave two people the opportunity to take charge of the kitchen. I went back to New Orleans, but I would still approve all the menus. I was able to monitor the progress of the two potential replacements by camera with a feed to my computer.

One of the chefs couldn't keep up with the rigors of supervising, so he didn't get the job. I was pleased that the other chef was diligent, and he demonstrated in every way that he could not only handle the job, but he would be superior at it. I gave him the job and was happy to promote from within for a lot of good reasons. The most important being the crew would not have to adjust to a replacement supervisor and the other way around.

President Obama and I would bump heads now and then. One of my issues was there was not enough being done for Veterans. There are too many homeless Veterans, and I let President and Mrs. Obama know how I felt. When I would bring the dinner in, I would talk to them. I believe some of my conversations got through because Mrs. Obama began talking about her initiatives to help veterans.

President Obama would take off his jacket and freshen up as was his practice before the meals. He would then come out to the dining area and sit down and talk. He always asked how my health was doing and the health of my wife and kids. He asked about what I was feeling concerning things in general and then in particular. He cared. He wanted to know how I felt about things as if I were the special one.

I never called the presidents by their first names no matter how close or comfortable I would be with them. Most of the time, I would address them as "President" or "Mr. President." I hate the way the enemies of our presidents treat them. The fact that any man has become President of the United States should be respected no matter how much we disagree with them.

I do have a love for President Obama, and it is not because

he is black. That's what people have accused me of, but they must remember that I have made no bones about the fact that Mr. Reagan was my favorite President, and isn't he white? The last time I checked, he was.

I admire him because he came from a meager existence, and the fact he had a dream and kept pursuing it until he made it. I had the same dream but in a different way. I wanted to be a doctor and then a chef, and I had dreams of someday being a White House Chef, and I did it. That's the closeness I feel to President Obama.

I told the President one day when he was the most vulnerable to hearing me that I had been privileged to make my mark, but I wasn't done yet.

"I have children I want to teach culinary arts," I told the President. "I want to pass this on and leave a legacy to not only my family but to kids around the world. I want to touch their lives. I want them to have Christian and moral values. Our kids need a sense of family and sense of economic responsibility, so they will never be homeless and broke."

President Obama listened as he always did with the courtesy of the gentleman he is. He relates to all the things I said to him. President Obama and family go to church. They don't get in a car and ride. They leave the White House walking to church, and the President holds his wife's hand. Mrs. Obama holds the youngest girl's hand, and Mrs. Robinson walks behind them. They are setting an example for all the families in America, but no one knows all this because the media doesn't care about it. The public should see the President demonstrate how much of his life, including the Presidency, is about family.

When I left the president and retired from my job and duties at the White House, President Obama did more than say goodbye to me. I would have been happy with a "so long," or I may not have been unhappy if he didn't say goodbye at all because he was so busy.

Not only did President Obama say goodbye, but also there are many treasures in my house that he gave to me as parting gifts to show his appreciation for what I had done. There are only three particular oil paintings in the world of President and Mrs. Obama, and one of them hangs on the wall in my living room.

The President had culinary pieces made that represent various things. One of them represents my wife and I. The piece is made from stones and seashells taken from the coasts of Africa that look like faces. It is the only piece like it in the world. He gave me a gift that he had made out of sterling silver. It is a bouquet of nine flowers with a larger one coming out of the center. These nine flowers represent my eight children and my wife. The larger flower represents Ann as the overseer of the children. It is beautiful.

Mrs. Obama presented me with a set of crystal glasses that were hand made in Paris. They were etched by hand with a twenty-two karat gold rim around each glass. Other First Ladies presented me with all sorts of gifts that would remind me of my time with them while serving as a chef at the White House.

Two more times President Obama asked me to stay, but I again told him that I had to go and take care of myself and enjoy my family. He said that if I had to go, they were sending me off right. He purchased a scooter for me to ride and had it specially built for my handicap condition. It cost twenty-eight thousand dollars and is candy apple red. It had to be red to remind me that I am an American, and my buddies shed their blood as millions of Americans have done throughout our history to preserve our freedoms.

President Obama called me before I left and asked if I would bake a cake for Mrs. Obama's birthday. Of course I obliged. Michelle Obama called me at home on Christmas Day and told me she misses me and wishes I would come back to the house. I didn't think it was she at first, so I gave her one-half of the passwords, and she gave me the other half. It was she, and I was thrilled that she would take her time one hour before her husband and her would walk to church.

She asked me what was going down with me. I told her I was thinking about writing a book, and I was building two culinary schools for children and handicapped children.

Mrs. Obama then said, "The chef you left in charge is in no way as good as you. No one can cook like you, Master Chef."

Mrs. Obama wished me a Merry Christmas and then called me on my birthday. She sent a special gift. It was an ink pen with my name engraved on it and the insignia of the President of the United States.

CHAPTER SEVEN
President Barack Obama's Favorite Meals
How He Liked to Dress

President Obama ate breakfast every morning at 7:28 a.m. His lunch was at 12:28 p.m., and his dinner hour was precisely at 6:28 p.m. The reason? He was elected in 2008.

Breakfast

President Barack Obama's favorite breakfast was an egg white omelet made with crumbled bacon and shredded provolone cheese. He had one slice of multi-grained wheat bread with raspberry preserves, and one banana. He drank coffee with no sugar and no cream – "Just like my wife," he would say.

Lunch

President Obama loved meatloaf served with a boiled egg in the middle, crisscrossed with thick bacon with orange marmalade preserves. We made mashed potatoes using Yukon Gold potatoes and sour cream. The vegetables were white and green asparagus. The salad was made with light spinach, fresh strawberries, blueberries, feta cheese, toasted pine nuts, and raspberry and walnut vinaigrette. For dessert, he had black cloud cake made with dark Belgian chocolate and King Arthur flour (use mayo instead of cooking oil, French unsalted butter, brown organic eggs, Mada-

gascar vanilla, Louisiana sugar, and Blue Plate Mayonnaise.
The President drank Obamanade. It is made with 2 liters of Vernors ginger ale, a quart of orange juice with pulp, 2 cups pineapple juice with pulp, and 2 tablespoons of freshly grated sugar. Mix it all and serve cold with no ice. President Obama drank this juice five days a week.

Fast Foods

When President Obama wanted some fast food, his favorite was Papa John's Pizza. He loved the shrimp pizza with jalapeños, red onions, extra cheese made in the crust, and black olives. He drank lemonade with no ice.

Favorite Alcoholic Beverage

Chardonnay wine from Napa Valley, California.

How He Dressed

You could often see the President dressed in a Navy blue suit, white shirt, and light blue tie. For casual dress, the President was comfortable in khaki pants, Air Jordan basketball shoes, and sunglasses. No shorts were allowed in the White House.

★ ★ ★ ★ ★

OBAMA

Menu

•

BABY SPINACH

Ponchatoula strawberries, fresh blueberries, feta cheese,
with a house-made walnut raspberry vinaigrette

APPLEWOOD BACON WRAPPED SIRLOIN MEATLOAF

glazed with orange marmalade,
side of white and green asparagus and pimentos

NEW ORLEANS STYLE BANANA FOSTER

with vanilla ice cream,
garnished with toasted coconut and a
banana liqueur/rum glaze

•

PREPARATION FOR FIVE PEOPLE

SALAD

2 lbs baby spinach
25 Ponchatoula strawberries
40 blueberries
½ cup toasted pine nuts
1 cup feta cheese
½ cup walnut raspberry vinaigrette
½ cup olive oil
½ cup apple cider vinegar
1 cup raspberries (pureed)
1 tsp walnut oil
Lemon zest (1/2 lemon)

DIRECTIONS

1) Mix olive oil, apple cider vinegar, walnut oil, raspberry puree, walnut oil, lemon zest, and salt together in bowl. Let chill.

2) Drizzle vinaigrette over stemmed baby spinach. Garnish with quartered strawberries, whole blueberries, pine nuts, and feta cheese.

3) Serve.

ENTRÉE

2 lbs ground sirloin (98% fat free)
4 boiled eggs
½ cup toasted bread crumbs
½ cup diced onion
1 rib celery (diced)
½ green bell pepper (diced)
4 cloves garlic (finely diced)
¼ cup brown sugar

½ cup ketchup
1 raw egg
½ cup orange marmalade
2 cups long grain rice
4 cups chicken broth
2 pinches saffron
2 tbsp unsalted butter
Applewood bacon
¼ cup olive oil
2 tbsp shallots
1 tbsp unsalted butter
1/8 tsp white pepper
¼ cup white wine
¼ cup heavy whipping cream
4 white asparagus
3 green asparagus

DIRECTIONS

1) Take ground beef and fold in bread crumbs, salt, red pepper, diced onion, celery, green bell pepper, garlic, brown sugar, ketchup, raw egg. Mix together, Keep peeled boiled eggs on side.

2) Place meat on cutting board and shape into loaf, take knife and open up in middle. Place 4 boiled eggs in middle and fold meat over. Place in sprayed loaf pan.

3) Melt orange marmalade in microwave, brush over raw meat and criss-cross aplewood bacon over top.

4) Bake in oven at 350 degrees for 60 min. Internal temp should be 155 when done.

5) While meat is in oven, mix rice, chicken broth, saffron, and butter together on stove on medium high heat w/ lid. Bring to boil and reduce to simmer. Cover. Rice is done when water has evaporated and holes show in grain.

6) To make béarnaise sauce, combine olive oil, shallots, 1 tbsp butter, white pepper, cook on stove top until shallots appear translucent. Add white wine and heavy whipping cream. Whip and reduce by half. Drizzle over rice and garnish with dill weed as needed for presentation.

7) Bend 1 asparagus until it breaks, use breaking point as reference and slice remaining stalks. Peel stalks and place asparagus in boiling water for three min. remove, pat dry, place on sheet pan and roast 5 min. in oven at 350 degrees. Drizzle with clarified butter*, add salt and pepper to taste. Arrange on plate according to colors.

8) Place rice on side of plate, meat loaf in middle. Rub oil around plate.

9) Serve.

DESSERT

¼ cup toasted coconut
1 stick unsalted butter
1 tsp brown sugar
1 tsp nutmeg
¼ cup banana liqueur,
½ cup 151 rum
4 bananas (quartered)
Vanilla ice cream (two scoops ea.)

DIRECTIONS

1) Pack brown sugar in measuring cup and place scoop in center of skillet. Cut butter into 1 tsp. measurements and place around brown sugar. Melt butter.

2) Add cinnamon, nutmeg, and vanilla to simmer. Add banana liqueur and bananas until caramelized.

3) Add rum, take lighter and ignite (for presentation, sprinkle cinnamon).

4) Toast shaved coconut on pan sheet in oven at 175 degrees until golden brown.

5) Drizzle sauce over ice cream, sprinkle with toasted coconut.

6) Serve.

EPILOGUE
Dr. Sherman Smith, Writer, Publisher

MEETING THE CHEF

I am a writer first and then a publisher. I have written different types of books and have been privileged to be a part of some great ones. Of all the books I've published, written and helped write, there is no book I found more fascinating than this one.

I was in New Orleans attending a contract celebration with Grandmaster Eric O'Neal. Heritage Builders Publishing had offered the Grandmaster an agreement to publish his series of graphic novels entitled *Lionman.* Eric is the seven times undefeated Champion of the World in Karate.

The celebration took place on the front lawn of a mansion on St. Charles Street in New Orleans. Grandmaster does everything with the highest degree of intensity, and this celebration was no different.

When I arrived there, African American people were everywhere, and I found myself the only white boy on the entire block. I was dressed in a nice blue suit with a yellow tie. The heat that day in mid-May was almost unbearable, but that didn't slow these people down. They were dressed to the nines just like me, and we were going to sign this contract and then celebrate, and celebrate we did.

A Bourbon Street band arrived by marching down the middle of the avenue and playing those blues songs, and I soon found myself with a parasol of feathers above my head and dancing like a fool. We danced and danced and sweated and sweated. I ruined a very expensive suit, but it was worth it. When would I have an experience like this ever again? I had only been to New Orleans once in my life and then only briefly. Now I was entrenched in this culture, and my life was about to change forever.

There was an African American gentleman standing by the way. He had on a white jacket, black pants, a very tall hat, and a very interesting gold medallion around his neck that was also a replica of a chef's hat. He was instructing a couple of people dressed like him about stacking donuts. I had never seen donuts arranged like that as well as many other hors d'oeuvres he had skillfully placed on the tables. The whole setup intrigued me because obviously this wasn't a wannabe chef that just walked off the street.

"How are you?" I asked as I walked up to the table and grabbed a glass of orange juice.

"I'm fine," the chef replied. "Aren't you the publisher?"

"I certainly am, and you are...?"

"I am Sir Master Chef Dr. Ronnie Seaton. Thirty-four years and five Presidents in the White House."

I was impressed. I had had only met one or two chefs in my entire life and certainly no one that represented food or kitchen in the White House.

"What is the that gold medallion around your neck?" I asked directly.

"Oh," he noted. "The Queen gave that to me."

"You mean like as the Queen of England?"

"Yes Sir!" The Master Chef exclaimed.

I was drawn immediately to him. "Why are you here?"

"Michelle Obama is having a dinner down here for around a hundred people, and she asked that make the meal." The chef in the big white hat explained smiling happily.

We talked for a while and then all the festivities began. After the dance, I asked if the chef, and I could talk. We walked under a nearby shade tree and tried to cool off a little.

"I'm retiring in a few months," the chef explained.

"What are you planning on doing after 34 years in the White House?"

"I'm actually taking an early retirement," he said. "I want to start a culinary school for children."

"What?" I asked incredulously.

"Yes, I have a passion to teach children how to make gourmet meals and to cook for their families."

Since I had never heard of such a thing before, I was fascinated by the whole concept.

"Can you imagine six year old kids making bananas foster?" The chef beamed. "I will need money to make this happen. We have had such devastation here in New Orleans from Katrina, and I don't think life will ever be the same. I want to help these young kids understand how a black kid from the hood could make it all the way to the White House and if I can do it, anyone can."

"Sir Ronnie," I said. "Do you have a book in you?"

"I am the longest serving chef in White House history. I have endured five presidents and 34 years. I have lots of stories."

"Would you be interested in a book?" I asked.

"Would I? But I don't write," he said sadly.

"Oh my friend, don't worry about that, I will write it for you."

Within a couple of months, I had made Sir Master Chef an offer. I flew back to New Orleans and ask Ronnie and Ann to have dinner with me. Ann was excited, and we even ate at an Egyptian restaurant where Xavier, the next to youngest son, was working as a cook and getting ready for college.

"What will you call the book?" Ann asked curiously.

"Sir White House Chef," was my reply.

There are books by a couple of White House chefs of the past, but I did not want a cookbook. We can do that later; I wanted something entertaining, and a book from the chef's perspective that would read like a novel. I didn't care if he could remember every date and event with pinpoint accuracy. I wanted his experience through his eyes and possibly tell a story that no one else would tell.

We can't put into words the life this man has lived. How many of us ever meet a White House chef? They are pretty much sequestered and classified, so their relationships are kept inside the walls. I wanted to know what really goes on in there. Sir Master Chef Dr. Ronnie Seaton was willing to tell his story.

He has another motivation. He wants to make enough money to make his dream of a children's culinary school a reality, and this chef can pull it off. He has begun already in humble beginnings, and I have seen children making a gourmet dinner. That had to be one of the most rewarding secrets ever revealed to me, and I want to tell the world to jump on board with this man. Poor children left in poverty because of Katrina are now growing up, and this African American chef who had a storied career as the longest tenure of employment as a chef in the White House can change their lives.

SOME INTERESTING THINGS

I became fascinated with the whole structure of the White House kitchens but more importantly the organization. Obviously, you could never work like this without structure.

Cook 3 - Known as a tournant or a swing chef. He will do any type of job needed in the kitchen from prepping vegetables to cleaning up.

Cook 2 - He starts cooking under a Level 3 Chef. This job requires the chef to put all the ingredients together to start the cooking. He also becomes a Saucier, or a chef who tastes the food in order to advise when modified adjustments need to be made to the recipe. In order to maintain and be good at this job, your taste buds must be ultra sensitive.

Cook 1 - Works under the Level 2 Chef and makes the pastries. This job requires the chef to be an expert at making cakes, custards, and almost every kind of pastry in existence. He also has to be able to make the perfect piecrust. He also must know how to make candy.

Chef Level 3 - Works with the Level 2 Chefs – He will be adept at sautéing, steaming, grilling, and poaching.

Chef Level 2 - Works with pastries. He gets involved with cake designs, and latticework on the crust of the pies. Crème Brule is also an art to make and has to be perfect when cooking in this environment. Ronnie says even though Level 2 is a very intense job, it is the best job in the entire kitchen. You're in a cool environment and when you're finished, you pass it on and get to go home. Everybody coveted that position in the kitchen.

Chef Level 1 - This is working with the Sous Chef. It is direct cooking with the entire meal under strict guidelines. You are learning how to cook the food and expedite it. The Level 1 Chef has to make sure that everything on the plate is perfect. It has to look perfect, smell perfect, and taste perfect.

Sous Chef - He is the second in command working directly under the Executive Chef. He is the quarterback of the kitchen. He moves around the food inspecting it, tasting it, watching everything that is happening. The thermometer is the most important tool in the kitchen, and the Sous Chef will make sure that all the food is served at the right temperature.

Executive Sous Chef - He is the manager of the kitchen. His job is to make sure that everything is on time and on task. He can hire and fire on the spot. He keeps the entire staff on point.

Executive Chef - The kitchen is his domain. He operates by communicating with only one person, and that is the Executive Sous Chef. His responsibilities include purchasing the food, is in charge of all the production costs, and takes care of the time sheets.

Master Chef - This is the most powerful position in the kitchen, and one of the most powerful of the entire White House personnel.

THE CHALLENGES OF MASTER CHEF

Master Chef Seaton retired a year early. He was intending to complete President Obama's last term but had to retire because of his medical conditions. Because of this early out, he does not receive a full salary but lives on disability income. When he reaches the age of 65, he will receive all the money that is in his retirement account. Until that time, he and Ann support the boys and themselves on the supplemental income he receives from this assistance.

Ronnie is a strong supporter of Operation Mainstream that teaches underprivileged adults how to function in today's world. He supports Make a Wish Foundation. He loves the concept of giving a child his or her last wish. He believes in giving back to the community. Each Friday, he goes and helps feed the homeless. His talents allow them to taste and eat superior food they could never afford anywhere else. He teaches "at risk" kids.

We hope this book sells really well because that will help his cause, and I am giving Master Seaton a very generous royalty. For what he has done and is doing for his community, he deserves the best that can be handed to him.

SOME PARTING THOUGHTS

As Ronnie and I were ending the recording of his stories, I had to ask about the Presidents' faith. The Foundation of the Founding Fathers had so much to do with faith in God that I was interested to talk to anybody that had the inside knowledge about how the Presidents worshipped that wasn't skewed by the media.

Master Chef Ronnie Seaton had seen it all. He would know, who was a hypocrite, and who wasn't. After all, he was with five of them and their families.

"What about President Ronald Reagan," I asked Ronnie. "Did he go to church?"

"Yes, he did," Ronnie replied with no hesitation.

"People I know that loved President Reagan believe he was a born again Christian. Would you say he was a born again Christian?" I asked.

"He definitely was," Ronnie said. "I don't know his heart of course, but I believed by his actions he was a believer in Christ as Savior. President Reagan was a President who prayed. He did it with us in his office, and before he ate his food. He gave thanks to God and prayed good prayers. People who don't know God don't do that."

"What about President George H. Bush," I began. "Was he a born again Christian?"

"President Bush went to church because Mrs. Barbara Bush made him go." Ronnie chuckled. "President and Mrs. Bush were prayer warriors. They believed in talking to God, and they did a lot of it."

"So, President George Bush is born again," I commented.

Sir Ronnie replied, "Oh my Doctor Sherm. He is a devout Christian, and it showed throughout his whole life. No one but a Believer could have the heart that President George, Sr. had."

I have to admit that after living in Arkansas during part of the Clinton years as Governor of the State, I was salivating to hear all about Bill Clinton's faith. He had a pocket full of controversies and rumors that followed him everywhere in that day and now. Did he demonstrate his faith?

"Okay, Master Chef, did President Bill Clinton go to church?"

The chef rubbed his forehead. "Oh my," he said. "President Clinton didn't go to church as much as the first two Presidents I served."

"Would you consider President Clinton a born again Christian?"

The Master Chef was having a tough time with this one. "His wife don't go too much," he mused. "President Clinton told all of us that he is a born again Christian, and I believed him. He prays and often prayed with us over his meals. He was ashamed of the fact that he was in the White House serving as president over people who thought God should be taken off the walls of the Capitol Building and our dollar bills. He never aspired to any of that nonsense."

I couldn't get the words out of my mouth about the next President when the chef interrupted me. "Oh, yes, the son. Yes indeed he is a born again Christian! Do you want to know why? Two words, Sherm, Laura Bush."

"Now, why would you say that Laura Bush would be the reason her husband was born again?" I asked.

"Well," he said as he rubbed his brow again. "That's not what

I meant. These First Ladies have strong influences over their husbands."

"That's a good statement," I commented.

"George Bush, Jr. may have some skeletons in his closet as we all do, but he adored his wife, and she kept him straight." Master Chef laughed at his own comment. "All jokes aside, I have heard President George W. testify of his personal faith and trust in Jesus Christ as Mrs. Laura Bush does. President George Bush, Sr. and his wife Barbara, President George Bush, Jr. and his wife Laura were the most Christian of the Presidents and their wives that I served."

"What about President Obama?" was my next question. "Does he go to church?"

"President Obama goes to church," Ronnie replied.

"Is he a born again Christian?" I asked.

This was the first time since we'd been talking and drinking a cherry coke that Master Chef hesitated. He seemed troubled.

"You want my honest opinion?" the Chef asked. "I don't know. I don't know. He does go to church, but that doesn't make you a born again Christian."

"It's time to change the subject," I commented. "People are going to want to know about Sir Master Chef Dr. Ronnie Seaton. Is the Master Chef born again?"

Ronnie stared at me and then those big brown eyes began to fill with tears. "On May 7, 2006," he began, "I woke up that Sunday morning with a heaviness on my heart. It was my birthday, so I decided that I would go up to the Baptist church near the White House. I sat down in the back and listened to the message. I suddenly got filled. The pastor asked if there was anyone in the congregation that needed prayer. He asked us to raise our hands. I did that, and he asked those people with hands raised to come down front, and he would pray for them.

I went up and knelt at the altar to pray. I became overwhelmed and started weeping. A gentleman nearby put his hands on me, and then said he felt something strong about me. He asked me where I work, and I told him, the White House. He asked what my job was, and I told him that I cook for President Bush. I explained that I work in Kitchen 2, but I cook for the President.

The man looked at me like he'd seen a ghost. He stood up and told the congregation that there's somebody special here today in the church. He then put a microphone to my mouth and instructed me to tell my story.

I told my story, and it didn't take long. He then asked me if I would like to give my life up to Jesus. I told him I was Roman Catholic, and I thought I already had.

He said, "That don't mean nothin. Your church ain't gonna send you to heaven. Only faith and trust in Jesus will save you from your sins and send you to heaven.

"I gave my life up to Jesus on that day and haven't been the same since. I go to both churches, Catholic and Baptist. I love the Baptists. When you go to an Orthodox Roman Church, sometimes people won't speak to you and when hands are extended just before communion, some people won't participate.

"That's not true with the Baptists. You walk into one of their churches, and people are all over you wanting to know your name, and where you're from. They shake your hand and talk to you like they've known you all their lives. Sometimes they have food and want a perfect stranger to sit down with them and break bread. And man, can they worship. They can sing like heaven's choir, and the preachers can bring up hell and put out the fire.

"The Baptists pray together and read the Bible. I was brought up in a strong Roman Catholic faith and never heard the Bible actually read. They read Misolets or little snippets of the Scripture.

"I had my ups and downs with the Catholic religion. All my life I had trusted my salvation to the Church and the Pope but not to the Lord. I realize that Jesus is the only door to heaven, and I accepted him as my Savior. I understood really for the first time what peace means deep down in your soul.

"I got sick in 2009. I coded. I was taken by ambulance into the ICU, and they induced me into a coma. I saw a very bright light and heard a voice as clear as could be."

The voice said, "I'm not through with you yet."

I stayed in a coma for five days and when I finally woke up, I had a tube down my throat and wires all over my head. My lung had collapsed. They had brought the priest in and told my family that I would not live. The nurses told me that my wife was in the room angry with God and beating on the bed. She was crying and begging God to not take this man from her.

"Why would you do this?" She would cry out.

When I woke up, there were men from the Knights of Columbus praying the Rosary, but I asked for my wife, and the nurse told me she was in the next room on her knees praying for me.

When I opened my eyes, they all started crying. They thought they would be going to a funeral but look at me now. I know I had an encounter with Jesus, and I'm alive to tell this story in this book."

Master Chef Seaton had several stints implanted in his heart. He lost the vision in his right eye, and his legs received severe nerve damage. He has braces on both legs and can't drive a car. He has every reason to feel sorry for himself if he wanted, but that is not our man.

"I am blessed," he explains. "God helps me with my recipes, so that when I feed people, there are smiles on their faces."

The Master Chef told me that he is so appreciative of my coming into his life because he had so many things pent up inside of him for so many years. As I worked through the life of this man, I understood that as a part of the public, I had no idea the sacrifices these people make for the presidents, the vice presidents, and the families of those men.

I didn't want to write or publish a cookbook. I wanted the public to feel the deep inward thoughts of a person who survived the rigors of a position and a job none of us know anything about unless we had been there.

Toward the end of my weeklong recording sessions with Ronnie, I sent out all sorts of emails and asked my family, friends, and employees that if they had a chance to ask the only American chef in the world that's ever been knighted by the Queen a question, what would it be?

Responses came from all over the country almost immediately. Dr. Otis Ledbetter, founder of Heritage Builders Global Ministries, sent this query: *Master Chef, out of all the good things that you did, what was your biggest failure?*

"So, Sir Ronnie Seaton, Sr. what was your biggest failure, and what was it's impact?" I asked. "You learn and become a better person by your failures."

The knight didn't even think about his answer. He looked at the floor and pushed the bill of his cap up towards the ceiling.

"I trusted somebody to do something I should have done myself," he said. "When I was with President George Bush, Jr., I decided to go shopping and buy a gift for my wife to celebrate her birthday. I left my Sous Chef in charge of taking care of something for Dick Cheney. My chef neglected to fix it exactly the way the Vice President wanted it.

The Vice President went berserk. The whole episode was over a BLT sandwich. The tomatoes had to be grilled on a grill; the lettuce had to be crispy, honey mustard dressing, and grilled chicken with Swiss cheese on Pumpernickel bread.

The sandwich came to Vice President Cheney on wheat bread. When he came to the Vice President with the food, Mr. Cheney said, "What kind of crap is this?" He wanted to know where I was. I got a call and was told to get back to the White House immediately because the Vice President needed to see me.

When I got back to the White House, I went immediately to the Vice President's office. He was furious. "What kind of crap are you trying to feed me?" He screamed.

I ask him what he was talking about because I had never served him crap.

"Well you served it to me today," he said

I asked to leave for a moment and headed down to the kitchen to talk to my Sous Chef. I asked him what was he thinking. "The production sheet clearly says Pumpernickel bread," I told him.

The Sous Chef seemed surprised until I showed him the production sheet. He declared that he'd misread it. How can you mistake Pumpernickel for wheat? I explained that Vice President Cheney is a stickler for detail, so the chef went up to the Vice President's office to apologize.

"It's too goddamn late, isn't it?" Mr. Cheney yelled.

While I was listening to the Vice President's rants over a sandwich made wrong as if a bomb accidentally blew up our kitchen, I made another sandwich. I did this so quick that the Vice President was startled by it.

"Master Chef, how did you do that so quickly?" He asked.

"Don't worry, Mr. Vice President, it will never happen again," was my response.

I learned a person should never leave something important for others to take care of while you're off doing something else. Vice President Cheney was as dangerous as a sniper on a rooftop. He was unpredictable, and I could have lost my job. As it was, my Sous Chef got demoted. He had to work thirty days without pay and no days off. Most chefs would have hit the road and not looked back, but this chef had integrity. He wouldn't let it beat him and stayed the course through the adversity. He learned from his mistake. I reinstated him as Sous Chef, and guess who got the job as my replacement?

We weren't dealing with a nuclear bomb; we were dealing with a bacon, lettuce, and tomato sandwich. It wasn't the element of the sandwich that made this situation so volatile. It was the reaction of one eccentric and powerful man. It wasn't the Sous Chef's fault. It was my fault leaving this touchy business to someone else. I knew what the consequences might be because Vice President Cheney was as volatile as that bomb. Mr. Cheney didn't believe in mistakes. He wanted perfection and made you pay dearly if you couldn't achieve it.

I survived all those years because I went out of my way to please everybody even when it grated on me sometimes to cater and pander to these people who actually believed they deserved to be treated like they were heads and shoulders above everybody else."

Sir Master Chef Dr. Ronnie Seaton, Sr. retired in January of 2015 as the last chef that worked for President Ronald Reagan.